Introduction to Making
Cloth Dolls

Introduction to Making
Cloth Dolls

Jan Horrox

SEARCH PRESS

First published in Great Britain 2010

Search Press Limited
Wellwood, North Farm Road,
Tunbridge Wells, Kent TN2 3DR

Reprinted 2011

ISBN: 978-1-84448-458-4

Suppliers

For details of suppliers, please visit the Search Press
website: www.searchpress.com.
Alternatively, materials can be supplied worldwide via
the author's own website: www.jan-horrox.com

Publishers' note

All the step-by-step photographs in this book feature
the author, Jan Horrox, demonstrating how to make
cloth dolls. No models have been used.

Printed in Malaysia

Acknowledgements

I would like to thank Katie Sparkes, my
editor, for all her work and enthusiasm;
Roddy Paine Photographic Studio for their
wonderful photography; Ray Slater for her
introduction to cloth dolls; and Justine
Williamson for her constant help and
support throughout.

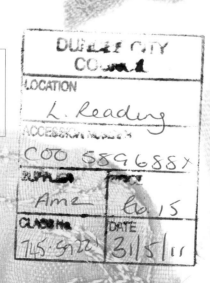

Contents

Introduction

Dolls have been objects of interest and creativity well back into ancient history. The modern-day cloth doll incorporates many technical skills and levels of design associated with the textile arts that are so popular today. For those wishing to expand their craft skills into cloth-doll making, or for those who wish to make a fairly simple cloth doll, you will find all you need in this book.

My personal journey began with a training in fashion/textiles, after which I spent a career in fashion design. I became captivated with cloth-doll making several years ago when looking for a new outlet for my particular experience and skills. Cloth dolls offer everyone an exciting opportunity to combine many varied craft techniques in one project, which will at the same time develop a fascinating personality of its own.

All the basic techniques for cloth-doll making are described in simple steps, with useful sections on hair, stuffing techniques, and hands, heads and faces. Some simple methods for fabric colouring are also included, with an emphasis on using recycled or everyday household items. Further instructions on embroidery and embellishment are included with each project.

The book contains three different projects for 40–46cm (16–18in) dolls, each with a second doll that is made using the same methods as the first but in a different colour scheme. The parts of all the dolls are interchangeable. The designs therefore lend themselves to interpretation by the doll-maker, allowing him or her to use their creative skills to develop dolls of their own.

Materials & equipment

To complete the cloth dolls in this book you will benefit from having the specified woven fabrics as well as certain equipment and tools. You can probably find tools from your sewing and craft equipment at home that you can use to begin with, while you develop your own style, and then choose to buy appropriate items that you will find invaluable.

I have used a fine, high-count woven cotton for the bodies of the dolls, and you will probably have a stash of fabrics and fibres that you can draw from for costuming, hair and trimmings. To create an exciting collection of dolls you will want to build up a diverse selection of small quantities of prints, silks, lace, novelty fabrics, ribbons and trims. Look out for interesting pieces at fairs and in charity shops to supplement your collection. Patchwork and quilting shops will stock a good range of prints and silks in fat quarters.

The tools and equipment specified in this section can be obtained from specialist internet sites as well as from some craft suppliers. Pens and pencils for face colouring can be bought from good art suppliers. Textile dyes and paints for colouring fabrics can be obtained from specialist textile craft suppliers.

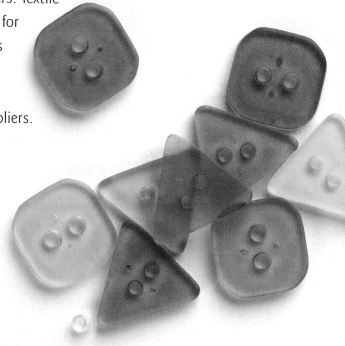

Materials for making the bodies and heads

I use a Pima woven cotton for the heads and bodies of the dolls. Pima cotton is a high-count cotton which has great strength and flexibility. It will mould easily into shape and makes a good, smooth surface for drawing and painting the face. It is also excellent for making and turning individual fingers. All the other fabrics I have used for bodies and limbs are strong, high-count, woven fabrics – these can be cottons or firm silks. Please make sure the fabrics you choose do not fray too easily, as this will lead to bursting seams. Egyptian cotton sheeting is now easily available and makes a good doll fabric. Of course, it comes in huge quantities, but perhaps you can share with a friend. Patchwork shops will usually stock good, plain, natural cotton.

Do not be tempted to use a cheap calico or a loosely woven fabric – this will not shape well or have the strength to hold the stuffing, and makes it very difficult to turn fingers. Many a good doll has failed when stuffed because an unsuitable fabric has been used – the body seams may fray, or the finger seams burst when turned.

Although I use woven fabrics for my dolls, some doll-makers use knitted fabrics. These are often used for character dolls, trolls, etc. You may buy cloth-doll patterns which cite 'craft velour' or 'buck suede' to be used for the body sections. These are both very suitable fabrics for certain types of doll. Knitted fabrics behave differently from woven ones, so it is advisable not to use a knit fabric for a pattern which asks for woven cotton and vice versa.

Assorted types of face and body fabrics in various flesh tones. A couple of knitted fabrics are included with a selection of fine-woven cotton fabrics. The three main threads I use for constructing the dolls are extra strong upholstery thread for jointing, quilting thread for needle-sculpting and polyester thread for machining. Use good quality super polyester stuffing for filling the dolls.

Decorative fabrics & trimmings

The costume and clothing for cloth dolls are not usually made separately – they are all part of the body construction. Skirts, ruffles, wings, beading, jewellery, ribbons and hair are all added to the doll when partly or totally assembled. Fabric colouring, painting and embroidery are applied to the fabrics before the doll parts are cut out and stitched together. This is the fun part of the process after you have put in the hard work of making the doll's head, face and body parts.

Polyester tulles come in many vibrant colours. Small pieces of polyester lace and cotton lace can be dyed and painted, and polyester ribbons in 7mm (¼in) or 3mm (⅛in) widths, available in a huge range of colours, make pretty additions to any costume. White ribbons can be painted with textile paint and then tiny buttons or beads sewn on them for decoration. Look out for novelty trims at sales and in charity shops. Often you can take something apart and re-use the pieces. Assorted beads, sequins and buttons will all add a sparkle. Angelina hot-fix fibres fuse together to produce a sheet of sparkling gossamer that is especially good for wings. It can be combined with sheer nylon organzas or tulles, and jewellery wire added for support.

Cotton prints, cotton batiks and dupion silks are available in a wonderful range of colours and designs.

A mass of brightly coloured polyester organzas and tulles for costuming. Look out for sequined dance fabrics.

Ribbons and fibres

Collect fancy printed ribbons
and trims for your stash. These
can be used to accent your
doll's costuming and can bring
the doll to life. Satin ribbons in
7mm (¼in) or 3mm (⅛in) widths
are available in a huge range of
colours. Angelina hot-fix fibres
make beautiful wings and can be
incorporated with other fibres.

Buttons and beads

Other items for your ever-growing
stash are all types of interesting
buttons and beads in a size suitable
for decorating cloth dolls. Look out
for these in specialist shops, charity
shops, craft fairs and on-line
auction sites, and remember that
old items of clothing and jewellery
are a rich source of interesting
embellishments for cloth dolls.

Hair

Hair for cloth dolls can be made from all manner of fibres, a selection of which is shown in the picture above. Those most commonly used are wool or mohair tops, dyed wool fleece, dyed mohair fleece and fancy yarns, which are very plentiful in craft shops. Old ribbing or fabrics cut into strips are also suitable when combined with a mixture of ribbons.

There is a particular type of yarn used by experienced cloth-doll makers, known as Yadeno mohair. It is a special, beautifully dyed mohair from Australian and Tibetan lamb skins, which comes in a variety of dyed colours, both natural and bright. It makes beautiful wigs, and is particularly suitable for fairy-type dolls. It is, however, fairly expensive and is only available from specialist suppliers, so for the three projects in this book I have used easily found and low-cost alternatives that can be just as exciting and attractive.

Colouring your own fabrics and trimmings

It can be very rewarding to colour or paint some of your own fabrics. This makes your work unique to yourself. There are many fabric paints and dyes readily available from specialist fabric art suppliers and also, quite often, from hardware shops. These usually come with instructions. Natural fibres, such as cotton and silk, are easiest to work with and give the best results. Experiment on some remnants of fabric before starting a whole project.

Painting ribbons and trims

These are fun to decorate by painting on stripes or stamping with stars, circles or other shapes. Pin out the ribbon to keep it steady and either paint on stripes or other shapes freehand with a paintbrush, or stamp on a design as shown opposite. When dry, iron on the back of the ribbon with a hot iron to fix. You can then add beads, buttons or embroidery to complete your unique trims.

Materials for colouring fabrics. These include hand-made blocks for printing (see below), various foam and stiff-bristle brushes and dyes.

Block printing natural fabric pieces

This method will work well for any natural fabrics, such as cotton or silk. Here I have used Jacquard textile paints in violet and Jacquard Lumiere in gold, and applied them to the block using a foam brush. Alternatively, you can roll out the paint on to a laminated sheet using a brayer (roller) and then dip the block in to the paint. Begin by covering your table with plastic. Use wet wipes for cleaning your equipment and your hands afterwards.

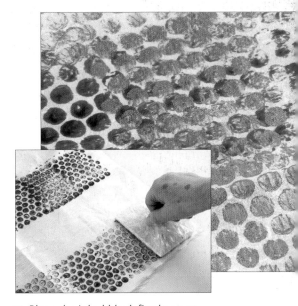

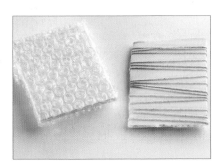

1 Make your block by wrapping bubblewrap around a piece of thick card or foam board, about 8 x 12cm (3¼ x 4¾in). Secure it in place and leave a 'handle' at the back. You may prefer to create a different type of block by wrapping medium-weight string around it.

2 Spoon some textile paint into a plastic container. Holding the block at the back, pick up some paint with the foam brush and paint it on to the block. Make sure the block is evenly coated with dye.

3 Place the inked block firmly on to the fabric. Repeat this as required to create your design. When the first coat is dry you can overprint with a second colour. When thoroughly dry, iron the back with a hot iron to fix.

Tools and equipment

Most of the tools and equipment listed below are available from general art and craft suppliers and haberdashery shops. The more specialist items can be bought from doll-making and quilting suppliers, including internet and mail-order companies.

Sewing machine

Your sewing machine will need to have an open quilting/appliqué foot or a clear foot in order to sew around intricate pattern shapes like fingers. Always use a small stitch size (1–2, depending upon the type of machine). This enables you to stitch around small pieces and also makes a strong seam.

Scissors

You will need sharp-pointed embroidery scissors; good, sharp fabric scissors for cutting out fabric pieces; and a pair of paper scissors.

Needles

Doll needles, used for jointing the doll together, usually come in sets of two or three and are approximately 18cm (7in),12cm (4¾in) and 7cm (2¾in) long. Long, fine darning needles, size 7, are also useful, and an assortment of long, fine darning needles in sizes 1 to 5 are ideal for sculpting the face. Felting needles, gauge 36 or 40, can be used for felting fibres into the cloth-doll head to make hair. You will also need a selection of ordinary sewing needles suitable for hand stitching.

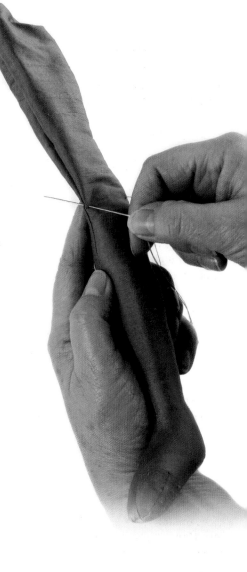

Glass-headed pins

These are used for marking the points on the needle-sculpted face before stitching, and for securing fabric, trims, ribbon, etc. before stitching.

Threads

You will need quilting thread for needle-sculpting the face and for ladder stitch (used for closing seams after stuffing); good polyester threads for machine stitching fabrics; and an extra-strong upholstery thread capable of withstanding the strain of jointing the limbs and body together – it can be mortifying if it snaps halfway through the process!

Forceps or hemostats

Hemostats (medical forceps) are an excellent tool for the cloth-doll maker. They come in a wide range of sizes, but I find about 12cm (5in) the most useful. Use them for turning the doll pieces, for smoothing through the seams when turned and for pushing stuffing into the difficult-to-reach places. Forceps are available from cloth-doll suppliers and fishing shops.

Stuffing tool

This is specifically designed for pushing the stuffing into the various doll parts. A chopstick is a good substitute to begin with.

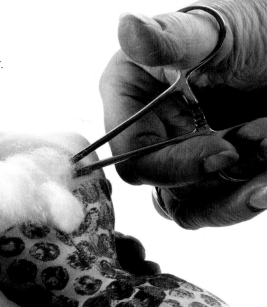

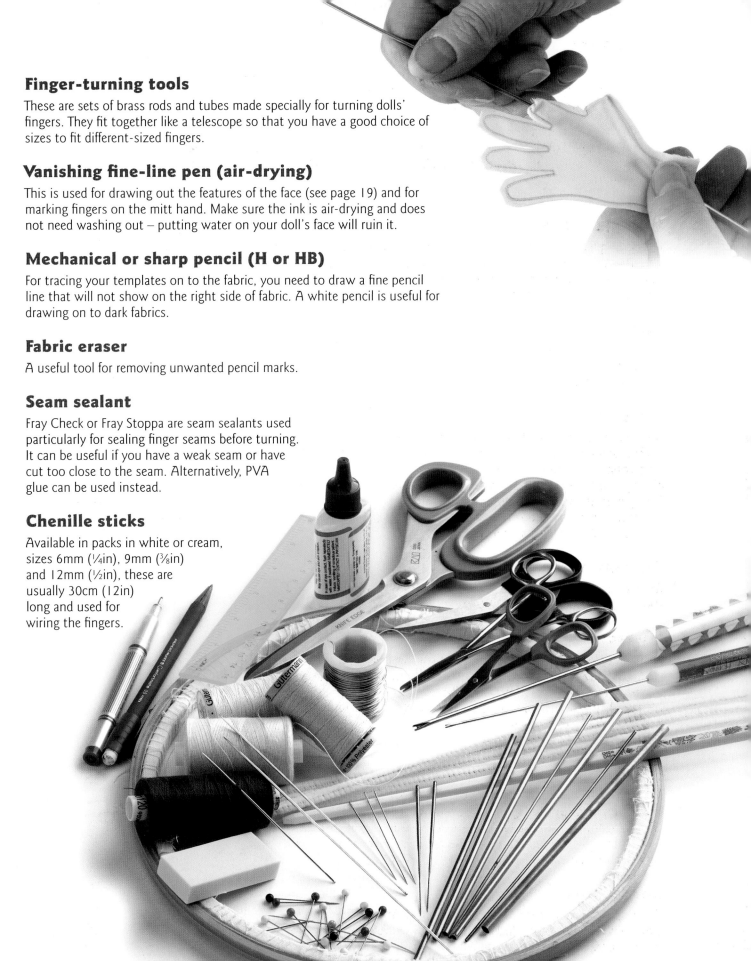

Finger-turning tools

These are sets of brass rods and tubes made specially for turning dolls' fingers. They fit together like a telescope so that you have a good choice of sizes to fit different-sized fingers.

Vanishing fine-line pen (air-drying)

This is used for drawing out the features of the face (see page 19) and for marking fingers on the mitt hand. Make sure the ink is air-drying and does not need washing out – putting water on your doll's face will ruin it.

Mechanical or sharp pencil (H or HB)

For tracing your templates on to the fabric, you need to draw a fine pencil line that will not show on the right side of fabric. A white pencil is useful for drawing on to dark fabrics.

Fabric eraser

A useful tool for removing unwanted pencil marks.

Seam sealant

Fray Check or Fray Stoppa are seam sealants used particularly for sealing finger seams before turning. It can be useful if you have a weak seam or have cut too close to the seam. Alternatively, PVA glue can be used instead.

Chenille sticks

Available in packs in white or cream, sizes 6mm (¼in), 9mm (⅜in) and 12mm (½in), these are usually 30cm (12in) long and used for wiring the fingers.

Face-colouring equipment

When starting to make cloth dolls, many people feel daunted by the face colouring. By following these instructions as carefully as possible you will be surprised how easy it is to achieve a good result. The more faces you paint the more confident you will become. Try to make three heads for each doll you make and then choose the best one. This way you will get plenty of practice and soon become very proficient in drawing faces. You can then progress on to developing your own style and colours.

It is advisable to use the equipment listed here to get the best results. Fine Pigma Micron pens will not run on fabric and the soft watercolour pencil crayons can be blended together to create a wonderfully artistic, coloured face using cotton buds or a piece of soft cloth.

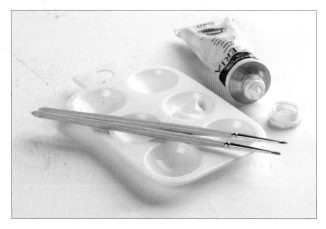

White acrylic paint and fine paintbrushes are used for painting eye whites and highlights on to your dolls' faces.

Artist's fixative spray is used for fixing faces after colouring them. Hold the can 25–32cm (10–12in) away from the face for spraying.

Watercolour pencil crayons

These are used for putting colour on to the dolls' faces, usually after the features are drawn in. They are softer than the pens and blend better on the fabric. I use them dry, not dampened. Prismacolour pencil crayons are very soft and blend beautifully, though they are not easily available. A good basic set to start with are burnt ochre, terracotta, goldenrod, grape, pink blush and cream for the skin colours; scarlet lake and crimson for the mouths; and a good light and dark blue or green for the irises. I also use dark umber, light umber, yellow ochre, carmine red, process red, magenta and white. As you gain more experience, you will develop your own preferred colour schemes.

Fine-line Pigma Micron pens

These are available in various thicknesses and are used for drawing on your dolls' faces. I use a size 005 (0.2mm) for the first outline and size 01 (0.25mm) for filling in when I am sure of the lines I have drawn. You need both these sizes in black and brown for outlining the features, and perhaps red for mouths and blue or green for irises, though all these colours are not necessary to begin with. These pens are waterproof and will not run on fabric.

Vanishing fine-line pen (air-drying)

This is used for drawing out the features of the face, so that if you are not happy with the result it will disappear and you can start again (see page 22). Make sure the ink is air-drying and does not need washing out – putting water on your doll's face will ruin it.

Making heads & faces

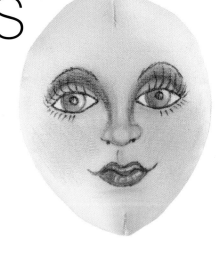

Miranda (pages 38–53) has a head made in three parts with a flat face. This head is simple to make and needs a little care when plotting out the face before drawing on the features. The other two dolls, Anastasia and Titania, have needle-sculpted heads, which gives them a three-dimensional face. The needle-sculpting is done before drawing the features.

Flat faces

Making the head

This type of head is made with three pieces of fabric. The front is one piece cut on the fold and the back is two pieces cut on the bias.

You will need

flesh-coloured fabric and matching sewing thread
templates (see page 88)
sharp pencil or mechanical pencil
glass-headed pins
small, sharp scissors
chopstick or forceps
stuffing

1 Place the two pattern pieces on double flesh-coloured fabric, with the Head Front piece on a fold, as indicated. Align the Head Back piece with the grain of the fabric as shown above. Mark around each piece with a sharp pencil. This pencil line indicates the seams.

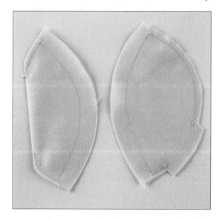

2 Machine stitch the centre back seam of the Head Back leaving the 'opening' unstitched. Stitch the darts on the Head Front piece. Cut out these two pieces with a 6mm (¼in) seam allowance on the side seams and 3mm (⅛in) allowance on the darts and centre back seam. Mark the side seams in pencil on both sides of the fabric.

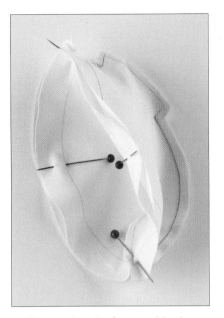

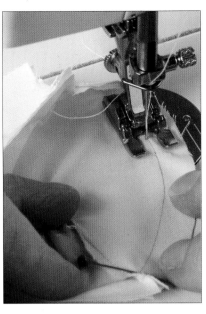

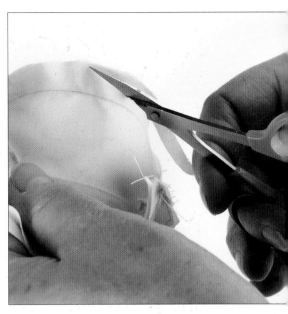

3 Pin together the front and back of the head, right sides together, matching the centre back seam and the centre front at the forehead and chin. Also match the sewing lines of the side seams.

4 Machine stitch around the side seam. You will now have a centre back opening.

5 Trim the seams to approximately 3mm (⅛in) using a pair of small, sharp scissors.

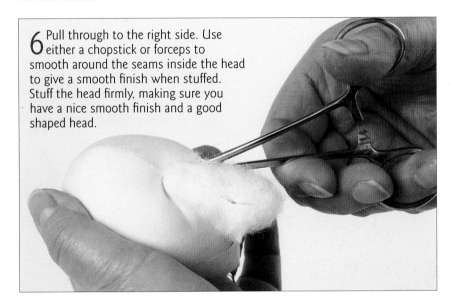

6 Pull through to the right side. Use either a chopstick or forceps to smooth around the seams inside the head to give a smooth finish when stuffed. Stuff the head firmly, making sure you have a nice smooth finish and a good shaped head.

7 The finished head. Pin together the opening – we shall be putting the neck into this opening when the doll is almost complete.

Stuffing

You will need either a chopstick or a stuffing tool for stuffing, and a pair of 12cm (5in) forceps. Use good quality polyester stuffing, which will not go lumpy. Start by turning the piece to be stuffed the right way out using forceps and flatten out the seams with either the forceps or a chopstick. This will help you obtain a smooth finish. Take a good handful of stuffing and push it into the centre of the piece to be stuffed using your chosen tool. The larger the pieces of stuffing you use, the smoother your doll is likely to be; pushing in small pieces at a time will tend to make your doll lumpy. Use the forceps to fill the edges of the piece, then keep pushing stuffing into the centre and teasing it out to fill all the crevices. The dolls are stuffed very firmly and you will be surprised at the amount of stuffing you will need for a fairly small piece. You are aiming to achieve a smooth and firm finish.

Drawing and colouring the face

The positions of the features are first plotted on to the face using glass-headed pins. This needs to be done carefully and accurately to achieve a realistically proportioned face. The features are then drawn in with an air-vanishing fine-line pen. If you don't like what you have drawn it will vanish in a short while. Use the pen lightly or the marks will take longer to disappear. Once you are happy with your doll's face, use the pens and watercolour crayons to colour the face permanently using either the colours specified or your own choice of colours. Blend the colours together by rubbing with a soft cloth or a cotton bud for a more painterly effect.

You will need

vanishing fine-line pen

glass-headed pins

Micron Pigma pens (sizes 01 and 005) in black, brown and blue

watercolour pencil crayons in dark and light blue, crimson, carmine red, burnt ochre, dark umber, yellow ochre, pink and white

white acrylic paint and a fine paintbrush

cotton bud or soft cloth

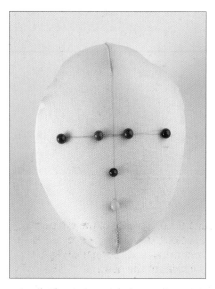

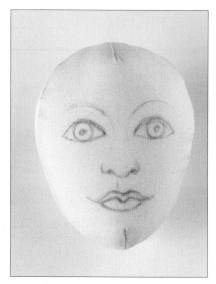

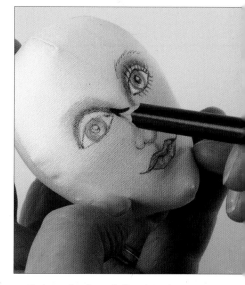

1 Begin by mapping out the positions of the features. Using a vanishing fine-line pen, lightly draw a vertical line between the two darts, then draw a horizontal line halfway down the face. Now you have a cross. Next insert pins as shown – evenly spaced on either side of the vertical line to represent the locations of the inner and outer corners of the eyes, and two more spaced evenly along the lower part of the vertical line to locate the centre of the lower part of the nose and the mouth.

2 Use the vanishing fine-line pen to draw the features on to the face. Position with dots the corners of the eyes and draw them in – first a circle, then the eyelid and then the iris and pupil. Next mark the position of the nostrils and then both corners of the mouth. Draw in the side flares and centre part of the nose, and the centre line of the mouth. Finally draw the upper and lower lip lines.

3 Colour the face, following the instructions opposite. Spray lightly with artist's fixative spray, held 25–32cm (10–12in) away from the face.

The completed face.

Tip

Before drawing the doll's face directly on to the head you have made, I would recommend that you draw a few experimental faces on paper as well as a spare piece of fabric to get accustomed to how the pens and pencils behave.

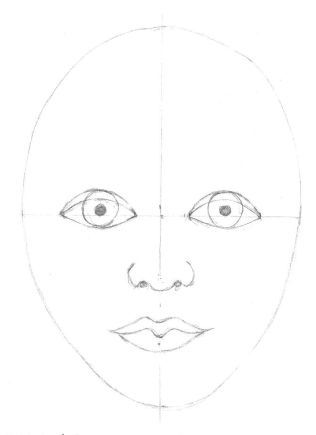

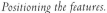

Positioning the features.

1 With the brown Micron Pigma pen draw over the three lines of the mouth and lightly fill in the nostrils.

2 With the black Micron Pigma pen draw over the lines for the eyes, eyelids and pupils. Fill in the pupils, leaving a white segment on the right-hand side for a highlight.

3 Outline the irises in the blue pen, though not the part underneath the eyelid.

Next you will add colour with the watercolour pencil crayons. You can blend the colours on the face with a small piece of soft cloth or a cotton bud. Rub the larger areas of colour as you go and this will blend the colours together smoothly.

4 Fill in the irises using straight lines radiating outwards from the centre of the eye. Use a dark blue on the left-hand side and leave a white highlight on the opposite side, next to the highlight in the pupil. Gradually blend the dark blue into a lighter blue as you move around the eye towards the highlight. Do not colour the part of the iris underneath the eyelid.

5 Use both reds for the lips – colour the top lip with the crimson (the darker red) and the lower lip with the carmine red, which is lighter. Leave white highlights as indicated in the drawing on both the upper and the lower lip.

6 Shade the upper part of the eye sockets, just below the eyebrows, with burnt ochre, taking the colour down both sides of the nose.

Colouring the face.

7 Use dark umber around the lower part of the eye socket, leaving the eyelid free of colour, to recede the eye socket and give the face a three-dimensional appearance. Again, take the colour down the sides of the nose.

8 Use white watercolour crayon on the eyelids themselves, the dorsum (the ridge of the nose) and the forehead to highlight these areas.

9 With burnt ochre shade the tip of the nose and the outside of each nostril. Apply the colour in a circle around the outside and gradually fade it out as you work inwards, leaving a highlight in the middle. Also shade one side of the philtrum (the area just below the nose and above the top lip), around the chin and down each side of the face. Blend the colour carefully to get a smooth transition between the different areas of shading.

10 Colour under the eyes and the top part of the forehead with yellow ochre.

11 Shade the cheeks pink and blend in the colour.

12 With the black Micron Pigma pen draw in the eyebrows using lots of tiny strokes.

13 Draw in the top and bottom eyelashes with the same pen.

14 Use white acrylic to paint in the highlights on the irises, pupils and lips, and to fill the eye whites.

Needle-sculpted faces

Making the head

This is a four-part head – two pieces for the front and two pieces for the back, both cut double on the bias.

I always make a number of heads at a time and keep them in a bag. I often go back to them later and choose a head which matches a particular doll.

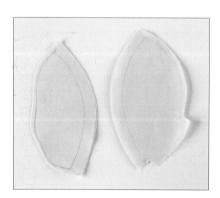  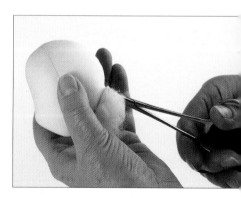

You will need

flesh-coloured fabric and matching sewing thread
templates (see page 90)
sharp pencil or mechanical pencil
glass-headed pins
small, sharp scissors
chopstick or forceps
stuffing

1 Place the template pieces on doubled fabric, aligned with the grain as shown on the left. Trace around the pieces carefully with a sharp pencil (remember, these lines are the stitching lines).

2 Machine stitch the centre front and centre back seams, leaving the back opening. Mark the sewing line in pencil on both sides of the fabric. Cut out the pieces with a 3mm (⅛in) seam allowance on the machined seams and 6mm (¼in) on the side seams.

3 Pin together the back and front pieces of the head, matching the seams at the top and bottom and all the side seams. Machine together the side seams and trim to approximately 3mm (⅛in) using a pair of small, sharp scissors. Turn the head right-side out and use either a chopstick or forceps to smooth around the seams inside to give a smooth finish when stuffed.

4 Stuff the head firmly and evenly, making sure the stuffing goes into the nose. When you think the head is stuffed sufficiently, close the opening with pins. Leave enough space to insert the neck when you are ready to attach the head to the body. You are now ready to do the sculpting.

Needle-sculpting the face

To needle-sculpt the face, follow the steps below. The sculpting stitches need to be pulled firmly to form the face shape, but not too tightly.

When first starting to needle-sculpt dolls' faces, you might find it helpful to make two or three and use the best one. It gives practice in making, and if one goes wrong there are still two more to choose from!

You will need

long, fine darning needle

quilting thread in colour to match fabric (natural is generally a good match)

glass-headed pins

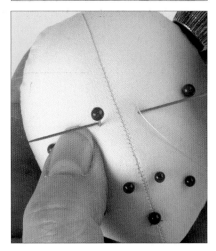

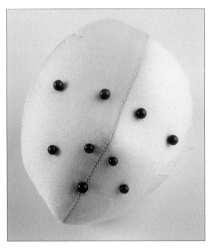

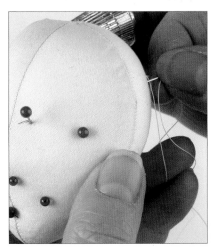

1 Mark the positions of the features with pins. This will help with the proportions of the face. Place two pins approximately 1.5cm (¾in) apart on either side of the centre front seam to mark the inner and outer corners of the eyes. Place two pins just below the tip of the nose for the nostrils and three below these marking the corners and middle of the mouth.

2 Thread a long, fine darning needle with about 1m (39½in) of quilting thread, and secure the thread at the back of the head with a couple of stitches. Push the needle through the head and out at the inner right-hand pin.

3 Remove the pin and make a small stitch by putting the needle back in as close as possible to where it came through, and take it across to the inner left-hand pin.

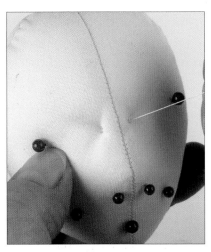

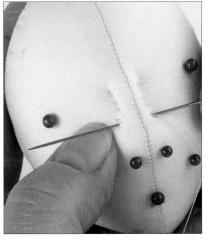

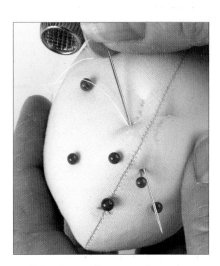

4 Pull the thread taut then repeat, making a small stitch on the left-hand side of the nose and taking the thread back across to the first stitch on the right. This forms the bridge of the nose. Repeat two or three times.

5 Continue down the nose, stopping on the left-hand side just before you reach the tip. With each stitch, manipulate the stuffing into the nose with your needle or fingers.

6 Take the needle across from the left-hand side of the nose and bring it out through the right-hand nostril.

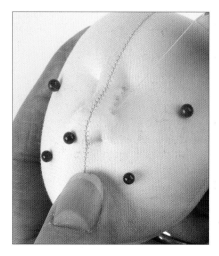

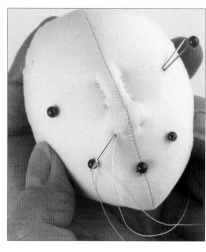

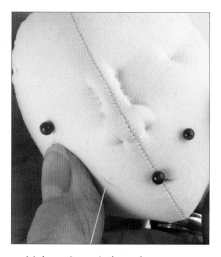

7 Pass the needle back through the nostril and bring it out through the lower right-hand part of the nose. Pull the thread taut.

8 Take the thread across and bring it out through the left-hand nostril, then make a small stitch and take the needle across to the furthest right-hand pin. Remember to remove the pins as you go.

9 Make a tiny stitch at the outer corner of the eye, and take the thread right across to the left-hand corner of the mouth.

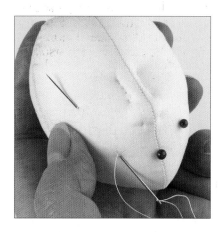

Tip

Remember that the sculpting stitches need to be pulled firmly to form the face shape, but not too tightly. Remove the pins as you go, leaving only the lower pin in the centre of the mouth in place at the end.

10 Make a small stitch and take the thread up to the outer corner of the left-hand eye.

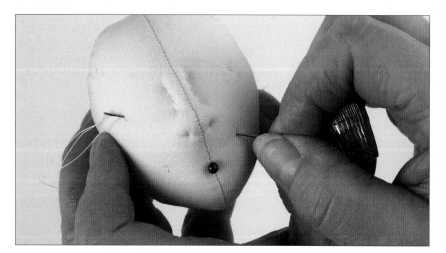

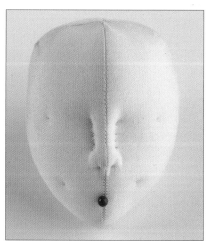

11 Pass the needle back through to form a small stitch and bring it out at the right-hand corner of the mouth.

12 To finish, take the thread through to the back of the head and fasten off. Leave the pin marking the centre of the mouth in place.

Colouring the face

This is very similar to drawing and colouring the flat face. In fact plotting the features is now made simpler as the needle-sculpting defines their positions. I have used different coloured pens and crayons for this doll, though the colour schemes are, of course, interchangeable and you can use any colours you choose.

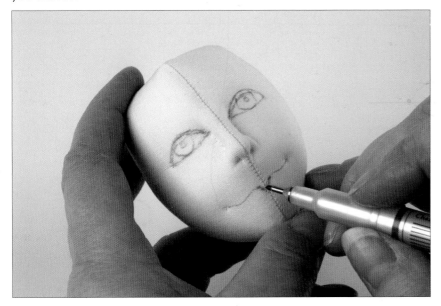

I Begin by marking out the features with a vanishing fine-line pen, using the needle-sculpting to get the position and size of the features correct. This face is very simple and as long as you get the features properly positioned to start with it is actually quite easy to get a successful result.

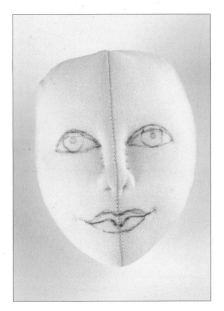

2 When all of the doll's features are marked in with vanishing fine-line pen, the face is ready for painting.

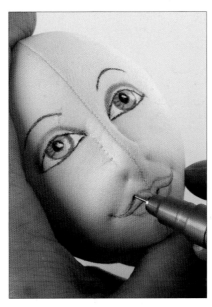

3 Colour the face, following the diagrams on the following page.

4 Complete the face and put to one side, ready for use.

Tip

Use artist's fixative spray to fix the face after it has been coloured. Spray lightly from a distance of 25–32cm (10–12in).

27

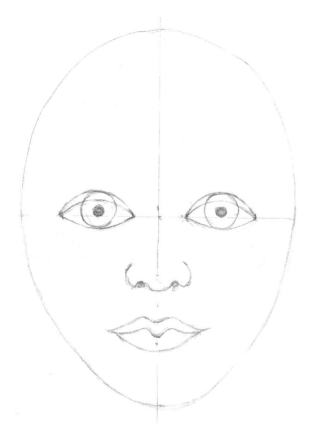

Positioning the features.

Colouring the face.

I With the brown Micron Pigma pen draw over the three lines of the mouth and lightly fill in the nostrils.

2 With the black Micron Pigma pen draw over the lines for the eyes, eyelids and pupils. Fill in the pupils, leaving a white segment on the right-hand side for a highlight.

3 Outline each iris in the green pen. Do not outline the part of the iris underneath the eyelid.

Next you will add colour with the watercolour pencil crayons. You can blend the colours on the face with a small piece of soft cloth or a cotton bud. Rub the larger areas of colour as you go and this will blend the colours together smoothly.

4 Fill in the irises using straight lines radiating outwards from the centre of the eye. Use a dark green on the left-hand side and leave a white highlight on the opposite side, next to the highlight in the pupil. Gradually blend the dark green into a lighter green as you move around the eye towards the highlight. Do not colour the part of the iris underneath the eyelid.

5 Use process red and magenta for the lips. Colour the top lip darker than the lower lip. Leave white highlights as indicated in the drawing.

6 Shade the upper part of the eye sockets, just below the eyebrows, with light umber, taking the colour down both sides of the nose.

7 Use grape to colour the lower part of the eye socket, leaving the eyelid free of colour, to recede the eye socket and give the face a three-dimensional appearance. Take this down the side of the nose also.

8 Use white watercolour crayon on the eyelids themselves, the dorsum (the ridge of the nose) and the forehead to highlight these areas.

9 With light umber shade the tip of the nose and the outside of each nostril. Apply the colour in a circle around the outside and gradually fade it out as you work inwards, leaving a highlight in the middle. Also shade one side of the philtrum (the area just below the nose and above the top lip), around the chin, across the top of the forehead and down each side of the face. Blend the colour carefully to get a smooth transition between the different areas of shading.

10 Colour under the eyes and the forehead with yellow ochre. Take the yellow ochre down the top of the nose.

11 Shade the cheeks pink and blend in the colour.

12 With the black Micron Pigma pen draw in the eyebrows using either lots of tiny strokes or a single thick line.

13 Lastly draw in the top and bottom eyelashes with the same pen – longer lashes along the top lid and shorter along the bottom.

14 Use white acrylic to paint in the highlights on the irises, pupils and lips, and to fill the eye whites.

Attaching the head to the body

You will need

forceps or a chopstick
glass-headed pins
quilting thread in colour to
    match fabric
long, fine darning needle

1 Take your finished head and remove
the pin holding the back opening
closed. With forceps or a chopstick
push a space into the back of the
head. Using the forceps push the neck
of the body into the space made in
the head. Make sure the head is the
right way round and straight.

2 Hold the head in place securely
and pin, turning in the edges of
the head opening neatly.

3 Ladder stitch the head in place
using quilting thread and a long,
fine darning needle. See pages 40–41.

Making hands

This section covers two types of hands: mitt hands with a thumb, and five-fingered hands including a thumb. Both have wired fingers and are slightly stuffed to give some shape to the hands, allowing you to make a pair of hands for each doll. Make sure you have one right hand and one left hand.

Mitt hands

A simple hand for a cloth doll is a mitt hand, which has a separate thumb and stab-stitched fingers wired with chenille sticks. This means they can be bent into position on the doll. I have used this mitt hand on Miranda.

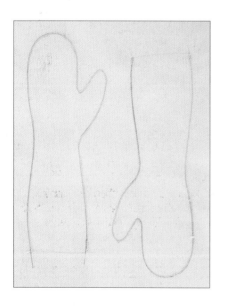

1 Draw around the hand and arm template on to doubled flesh-coloured fabric using a sharp pencil. Using a small stitch size (1–2), machine stitch on the line leaving the ends of the arms open.

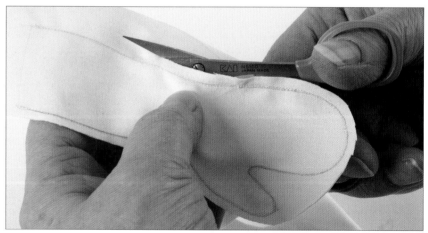

2 With the small scissors trim around the seams leaving a 3mm (⅛in) allowance. Do not trim the fabric between the thumb and the hand at this stage.

3 Put a dab of seam sealant on both sides of the fabric between the thumb and the hand and allow to dry. With small, sharp scissors snip down between the thumb and the hand. Get as close as possible to the stitches of the seam, being careful not to snip through them. If you don't snip close enough to the seam you will end up with wrinkles around the thumb when you pull the hand through. Trim away some of the excess fabric between the thumb and hand and pull the hand through to the right side with forceps.

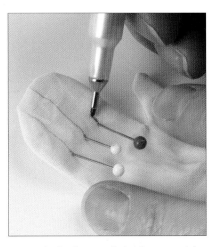

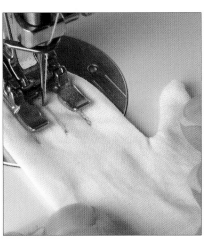

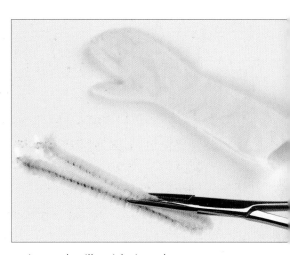

4 Mark the bases of the fingers with pins and draw in the fingers using a vanishing fine-line pen.

5 Remove the pins and machine stitch down the sides of the fingers. Fasten off at the base of each one.

6 Insert chenille sticks into the fingers and thumb to give them body and shape. Cut three chenille sticks in half and turn down the sharp ends with your forceps. Bend all six pieces in half again.

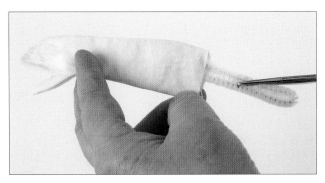

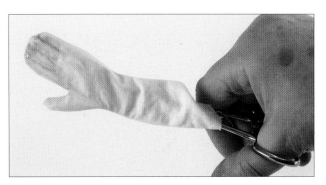

7 Using the forceps, push one folded chenille stick into the first two fingers of one hand (one half of the folded stick into each finger) and repeat for the next two fingers. Do this for both hands.

8 You now have two folded pieces of chenille stick left. Insert one into the thumb of each hand with the 'bend' going in first. Twist all the ends together at the wrist.

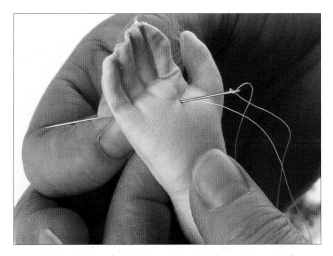

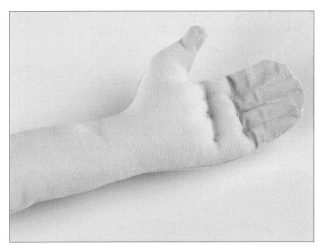

9 Stuff the palm of each hand, creating a right and left hand. Put two or three stab stitches near the base of each finger to give the hand a more realistic form. Now you can bend the hand into a natural shape.

The completed hand.

Five-fingered hands

Hands with separate fingers are more awkward to make and may need
some practice to achieve, but the results are rewarding. They are also wired
with chenille sticks and can therefore be posed. Some colour can be added
and nails drawn on after they are made. I have used five-fingered hands on
Anastasia and Titania.

You will need

flesh-coloured fabric and matching
    sewing thread
template (see page 91)
sharp pencil or mechanical pencil
small, sharp scissors
12cm (5in) forceps
finger-turning tools
3 x 30cm (12in) long chenille sticks,
    6 or 9mm
long, fine darning needle, size 7
quilting thread in colour to
    match fabric
seam sealant, (or PVA glue)
small amount of stuffing

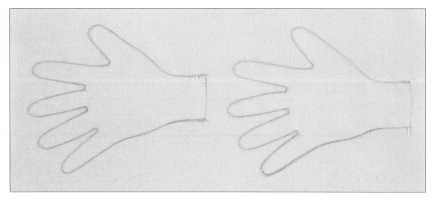

1 Using the template provided, draw the outlines for the hands on to doubled
fabric using a sharp pencil. Using a stitch size 1–2, machine stitch around
the hand leaving the wrist open. Make sure you have two stitches between each
finger to enable successful turning.

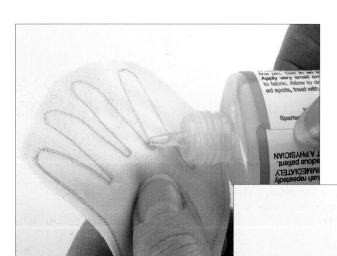

2 Cut around each hand using a pair of small, sharp
scissors, but do not cut in between the individual
fingers. Trim the seams to 3mm (⅛in). Put a dab of seam
sealant or PVA glue on to the fabric between each finger
on both sides.

3 Allow to dry, then snip to
the seam between each
finger. The closer to the seam
you cut the better the fingers
will look, but take care not to
snip through the stitches.

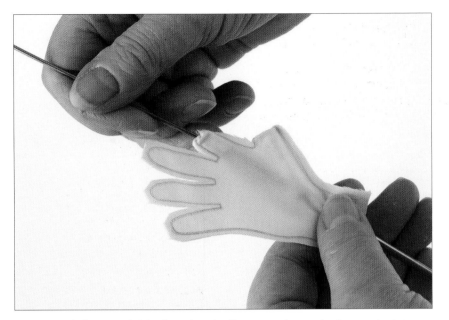

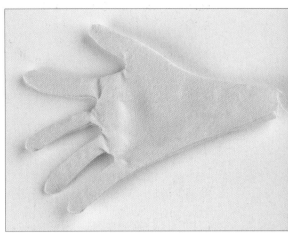

4 Turn each finger individually using the finger-turning tools. Put a tube into a finger and hold it in place by placing the rod slightly into the top of the tube. Push the fabric of the finger up over the rod. This will take a little time and patience.

5 When all the fingers are turned pull the hand through with your forceps.

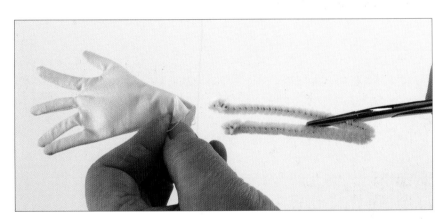

6 Cut all three chenille sticks in half, turn down the ends using the forceps so they are blunt and fold them in half. Use the forceps to insert one folded chenille stick into the first two fingers, pushing one half of the stick into each finger.

7 Repeat for the other two fingers. Push both halves of a folded chenille stick into the thumb, with the 'bend' inserted first. Repeat for the other hand.

9 Put a little stuffing into the palm of the hand with forceps and put in a few small sculpting stitches to form the knuckles and wrist, giving the hand a little more shape.

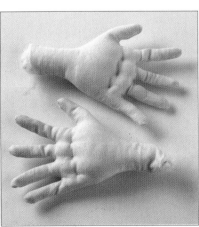

8 Twist all the chenille sticks together at the wrist.

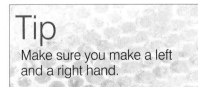

Tip

Make sure you make a left and a right hand.

Making feet

A foot can be a simple shape made as part of the leg, as for Miranda, or it can be further developed and made separately, with individual toes stab-stitched in after the foot is turned, and inserted into the leg at the ankle. This type of foot is used on Anastasia and Titania.

Making separate feet

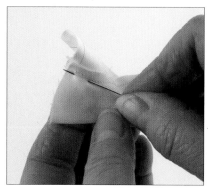

1 Mark the template for the foot on to doubled flesh-coloured fabric twice and machine stitch along the side seams using stitch size 1–2. Cut each one out, leaving a seam allowance of 3mm (⅛in).

2 Fold each foot with the two side seams together and pin in place.

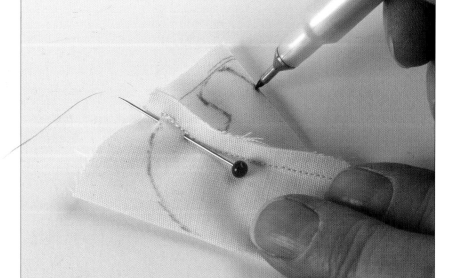

3 Use the vanishing fine-line pen to draw in the shape of the toes – a single curve for the four small toes and a separate big toe.

4 Machine stitch along the drawn line.

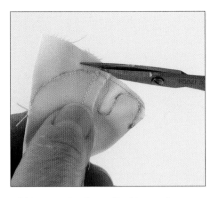

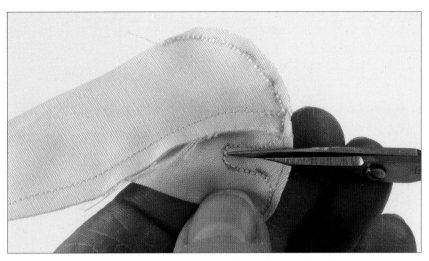

5 Use a pair of small, sharp scissors to trim around the ends of the toes, leaving a narrow seam allowance of about 3mm (⅛in). Add a dab of seam sealant between the big toe and the rest of the foot.

6 Snip down in between the big toe and the rest of the foot. Snip down as close as possible to the seam but without cutting through the stitching.

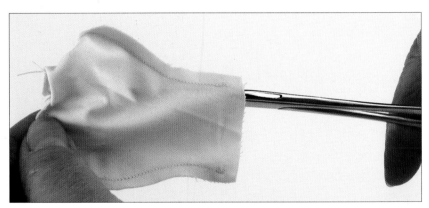

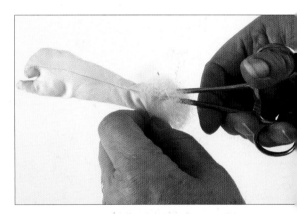

7 Use the forceps to pull the foot through to the right side.

8 Stuff the foot firmly using the forceps, pushing the stuffing into the big toe.

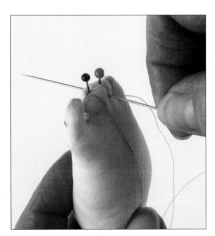

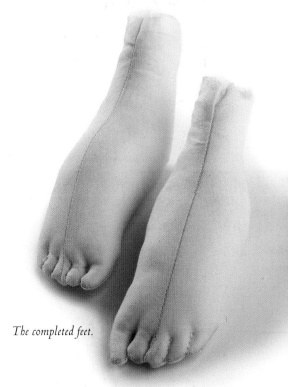

9 Mark the positions of the four small toes with pins inserted into the end of the foot, and draw in the toes using the vanishing fine-line pen.

10 Stab stitch along the lines using a long, fine darning needle and quilting thread. Start at the base of each toe, and when you reach the end stitch over the top of the toe and pull the thread taut to shape it.

The completed feet.

PROJECTS

This book contains three different dolls for you to make. Each one uses a different construction method and varied embellishments. The first doll, Miranda, is a simple doll for beginners. She has a flat face, mitt hands and stitched joints. The second doll, Anastasia, is a fixed-pose doll with a needle-sculpted head and five-fingered hands. Her limbs and costume are decorated with free machine embroidery. The third doll, Titania, has tab joints, a sculpted head and five-fingered hands. She has optional block-printed body fabric, wings made from Angelina and a beaded tiara.

The methods for making the heads, faces, hands and feet are all detailed in the previous sections of the book and you should refer back to these. All the templates are provided at the back of the book and are interchangeable from doll to doll as they are all made to the same scale.

Each doll can be customised by following the same set of instructions but changing the colours, fabrics and trims used. I have therefore included an alternative design at the end of each project which shows you how a very different looking doll can be made by using the same templates and instructions.

Before you start …

All the lines on the templates are the sewing lines, to which you need to add a seam allowance. The seam allowance for a stitched seam is 3mm (⅛in) and for a seam to be sewn after cutting the allowance is 6mm (¼in). In most cases you will trace the templates on to double fabric with a mechanical pencil, machine stitch along the pattern line and then cut out. There are specific instructions with each project where this may vary. Use the open appliqué foot on your sewing machine and a small stitch size (about 1–2, depending upon the type of machine). This enables you to stitch around small pieces and also makes a strong seam.

Miranda

This is a simple doll to make, with a flat face and mitt hands. She is fully jointed with stitched joints. Either follow the colour scheme shown here, or choose your own colour scheme from your fabric stash. Lay out all your suitable fabric pieces and trims to make your selection. You will probably find that you will change your mind as you put the doll together, but you need a 'colour story' to begin.

Head

Make the head and colour the face following the instructions for a flat face on pages 20–23. Put to one side while you make the rest of the doll. Hold the opening for the neck closed with pins.

You will need

templates (pages 88–89)

flesh-coloured cotton fabric: 0.25m (10in)

woven cotton or dupion silk fabric: 10 x 30.5cm (4 x 12in) dark orange for sleeves, 0.25m (10in) cerise for body; 0.25m (10in) blue for legs

polyester tulle in yellow and red: 0.5m (20in) of each colour

silver net: 0.25m (10in)

multi-coloured dyed habotai silk: 0.5m (20in)

7mm satin ribbon in red and purple: 2m (80in) of each colour

striped or painted ribbon for bodice trim: 45cm (18in)

small 6mm buttons or beads for trims

2 balls of fancy yarns for hair

4 x 15mm two-hole buttons for jointing

sewing machine with open-toe quilting foot and new needle

3 x 6mm (¼in) chenille sticks

250g (½lb) bag of polyester stuffing

polyester threads for machine stitching in colours to match the fabrics

extra strong upholstery thread for jointing

quilting thread for closing seams after stuffing

12cm (5in) forceps or hemostats

hand-sewing needles

long doll needles for jointing

long, fine darning needle, size 7

sharp embroidery scissors, fabric scissors and paper scissors

glass-headed pins

chopstick or stuffing tool

sharp pencil or mechanical pencil

vanishing fine-line pen

seam sealant (or PVA glue)

face-colouring equipment (see pages 18–19)

Body

The body is made from a piece of flesh-coloured cotton for the top section and plain cerise silk for the lower part. Pay particular attention to the neck, shoulders and hips when stuffing as these parts take the strain of jointing and holding the head and need to be strong.

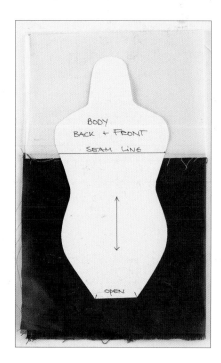

2 Prepare a piece of flesh-coloured cotton 30 x 10cm (11¾ x 4in) and a piece of cerise silk 30 x 15cm (11¾ x 6in). The grain should run with the 10cm (4in) and 15cm (6in) sides. Seam the two pieces together along the 30cm (11¾in) side. Press the seam on to the silk side so that it does not show through the flesh-coloured section. Fold this piece in half with the seam horizontal and the right sides together. Place the template for the body piece on to the fabric, with the horizontal dashed line on the template on the seam line of the fabric.

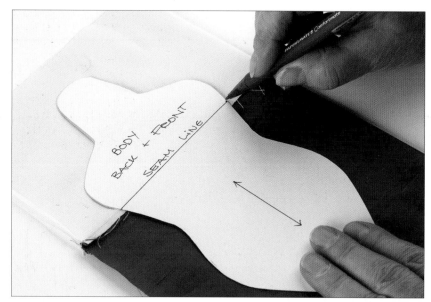

3 Trace all round this pattern with a sharp pencil.

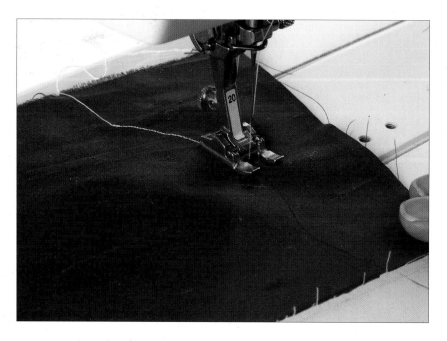

4 Machine stitch around the body on the pencil line, but leave the opening at the bottom of the body as marked on the pattern. Use flesh-coloured thread and small (size 1–2) stitches.

Ladder stitch

This stitch is used to close the openings in seams after stuffing a piece. Use a normal sewing needle and some polyester thread in a colour that matches the fabric. Fasten the thread at the beginning of the opening, then go in at 1 and out at 2, etc., as in the diagram. Pull the thread taut every few stitches and the opening will close up invisibly.

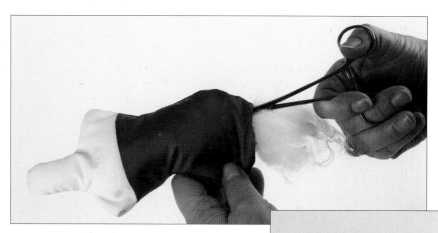

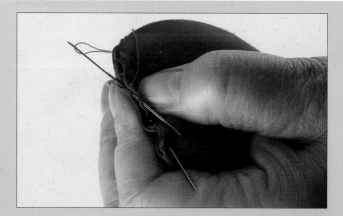

5 Cut out the body with a 3mm (1/8in) seam allowance. Make the allowance for the opening 6mm (1/4in) as it needs to be turned in after stuffing. Do not clip the seams.

6 Turn the body in the right way and stuff (see page 21). Take a good handful of stuffing and start to fill the neck first, then fill the body cavity. Push the stuffing into the shoulders and hips to make them very firm. This is important as they must be strong enough to hold the jointing of the limbs. If the body is too soft the arms and legs will not sit properly when jointed on. When you are satisfied with the stuffing, close the opening by pushing in the seam allowance and hold it in place with pins before ladder stitching.

7 Make the trim for the bodice. Wrap two pieces of striped ribbon around the body, one slightly overlapping the other, so that they cover the bodice seam. Pin them in place. Stitch on the buttons – one in each coloured section of the ribbon. These will hold the ribbons in place. Sew the buttons on two at a time, taking the needle and thread through from one side of the body to the other and attaching a button on each side.

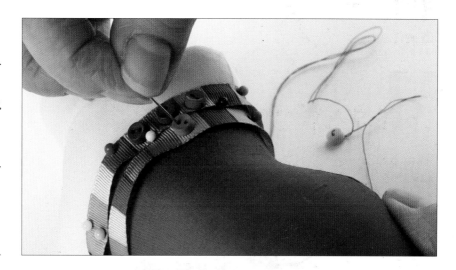

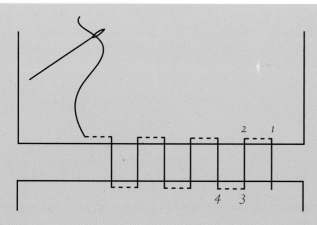

Legs

These are both made the same, from a piece of bright blue dupion silk.

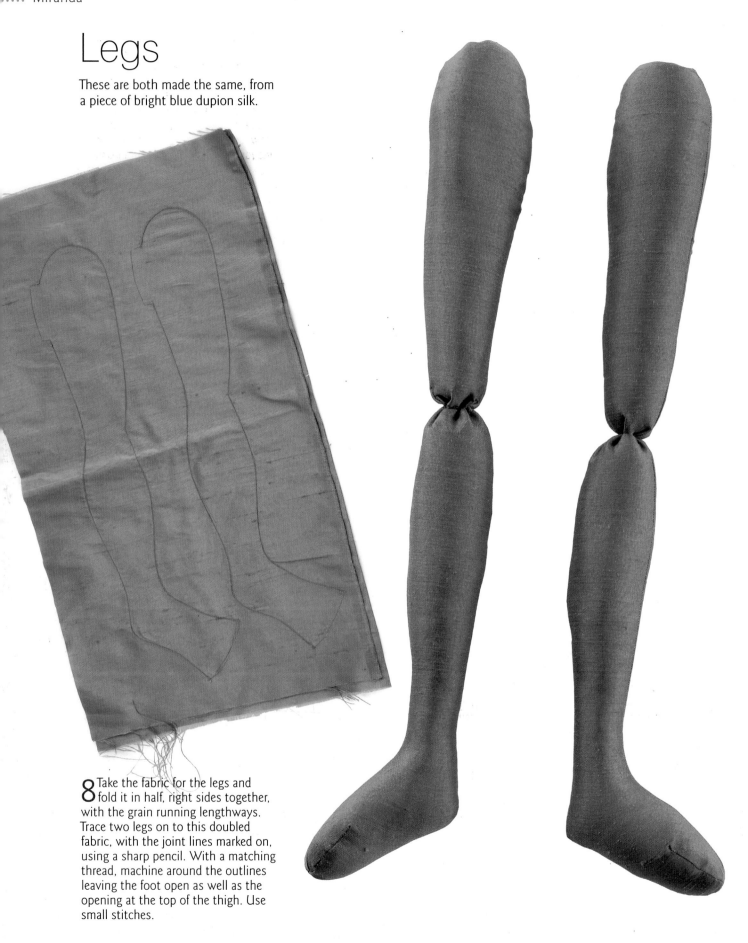

8 Take the fabric for the legs and fold it in half, right sides together, with the grain running lengthways. Trace two legs on to this doubled fabric, with the joint lines marked on, using a sharp pencil. With a matching thread, machine around the outlines leaving the foot open as well as the opening at the top of the thigh. Use small stitches.

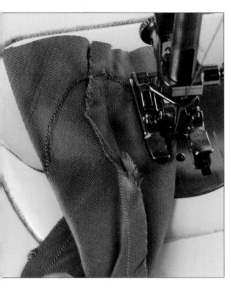

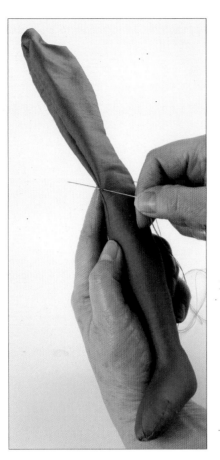

9 Cut out the legs with a 3mm (⅛in) seam allowance. Re-fold each foot with the back and front seams on top of one another and draw a neat, rounded shape on to each foot using a sharp pencil. Machine stitch along this line and trim the seam around each foot to 3mm (⅛in).

10 Turn each leg right-side out and smooth the seams on the inside, especially around the foot. Stuff the foot and ankle firmly, using the forceps to get the stuffing right into the toe. Make sure the ankle is very firm. Stuff the leg up to 1cm (½in) below the knee joint mark. Make the knee joint following the instructions below. Because you did not stuff right up to the knee joint, the lower leg can move freely.

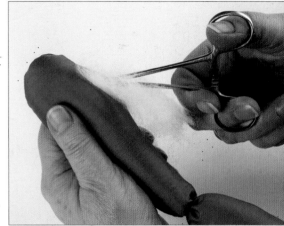

11 Stuff the remainder of the leg firmly. Tuck in the seam allowance at the opening and close it with ladder stitch (see pages 40–41).

Making a knee joint or elbow

To make a knee joint or elbow, take a length of doubled polyester thread in a colour that matches the fabric and a hand-sewing needle. Join the thread to the seam at the back of the leg with a couple of stitches (1). Next, take the thread through the leg to the front and make a small stitch, then take the thread round the leg and make another stitch at the back (2). Pull the thread tight to form the joint. Wind the thread tightly around the joint two or three times and finish off securely (3).

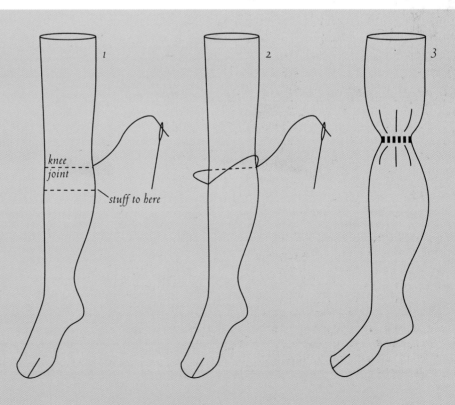

Arms and hands

Like the body, the arms are made from two pieces of fabric stitched together – dark orange at the top to make the sleeves, and flesh-coloured at the bottom for the lower arms.

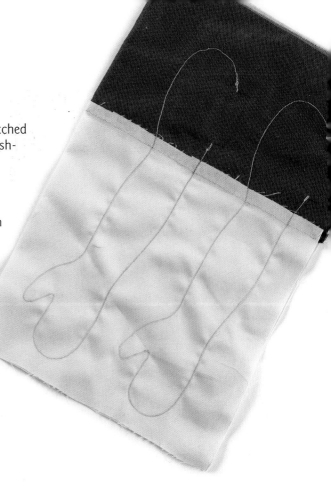

12 Start by joining two fabric pieces together, as for the body (see page 40). You will need a piece of flesh-coloured cotton 30 x 15cm (12 x 6in) and a piece of dark orange silk, 30 x 10cm (12 x 4in) for the top of the arm. The grain should run along the shorter sides. Seam together the 30cm (12in) sides and press the seam down so that it lays over the coloured fabric. Fold the fabric piece in half with the seam horizontal and the right sides together. Place the template for the arm on the fabric, with the horizontal line on the template aligned with the seam. Leave enough room for a second arm to be positioned alongside it. Draw around the template using a sharp pencil, then transfer a second arm in the same way. Machine stitch around both arms using flesh-coloured thread, leaving the opening.

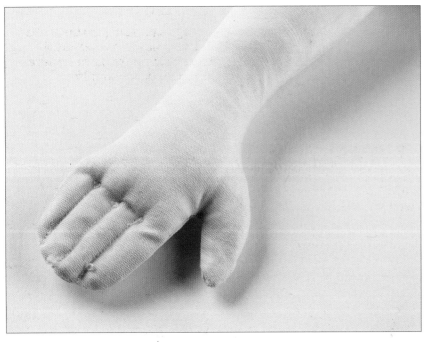

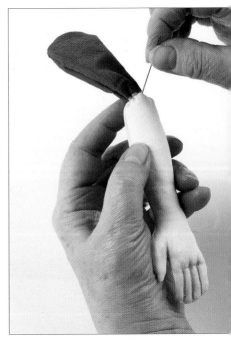

13 Cut out both arms with a 3mm (⅛in) seam allowance. Leave a little more around the opening flap. Make the hands following the instructions for mitt hands on pages 30–31. Stuff the lower part of each arm. Push the stuffing into the hand and wrist first and make sure they are shaped nicely. Put more stuffing into the palm of each hand, ensuring you make a left and a right hand. Fill the lower arm to 1cm (½in) below the seam line.

14 Make the elbow joint on the seam line where the two fabrics are joined. Follow the instructions on page 43. Because you did not stuff right up to the seam the arm can move freely. Finish stuffing the upper arm, close the opening and push the turnings well in. Ladder stitch to close (see pages 40–41).

Jointing the legs to the body

You will need two 15mm (¾in) buttons, a long doll needle for jointing and about 1m (40in) of extra strong upholstery thread. The legs are button jointed to the body on either side of the hips.

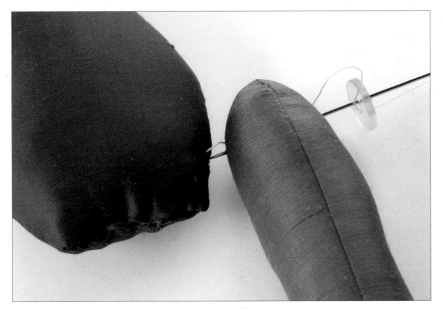

15 Attach the thread to one hip of the doll's body with two or three small stitches. Push the needle through the top of the leg and then the button, then back through the button and the leg to the body.

16 Continue to push the needle through the lower part of the body, coming out in the same position on the other hip.

17 Take the needle through the other leg, button and back again. Pull this thread to keep a firm tension but take care not to snap the thread.

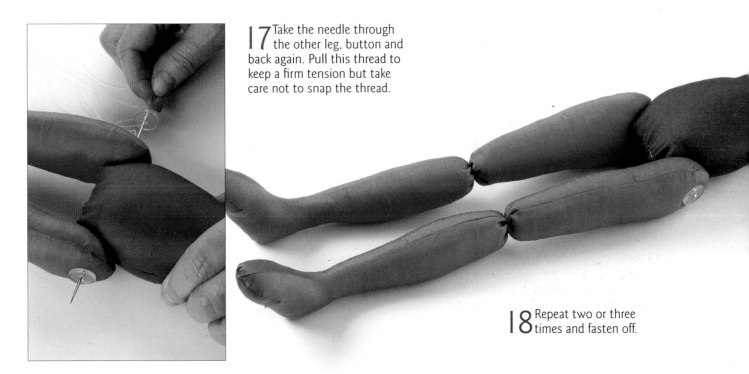

18 Repeat two or three times and fasten off.

Jointing the arms to the body

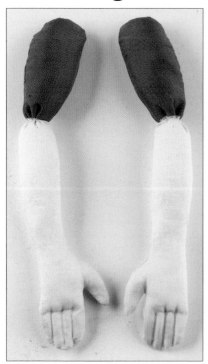

19 The arms are button jointed to the body in the same way as the legs. Attach them to the sides of the body, so that the tops of the arms are level with the shoulders.

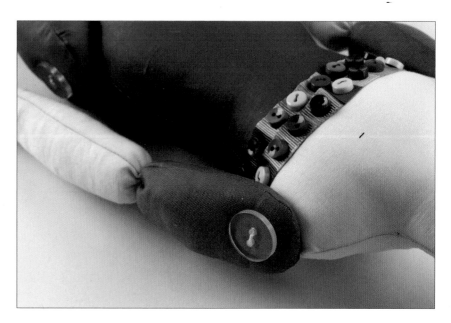

Attaching the head

20 Attach the head to the body firmly (see page 29). Remove the pins from the opening at the back. Using forceps or a chopstick, make a good space in the back of the head. Push the neck into the head so that the face is nicely positioned. Pin it in place and ladder stitch securely. Your doll is now ready to dress.

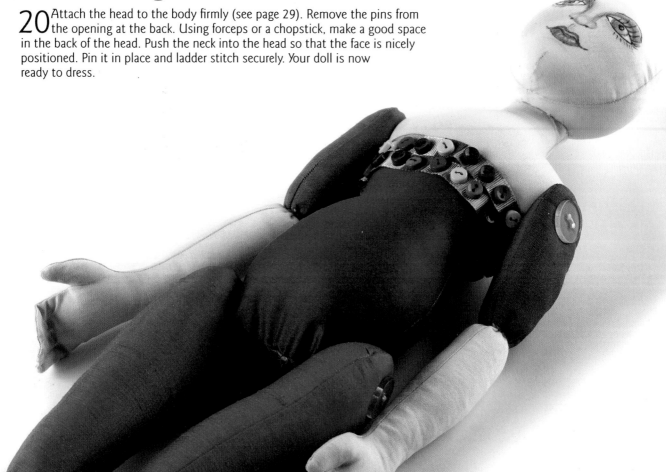

Skirt

The skirt is made from four layers of polyester tulle in two colours – three layers of yellow and a single layer of red. You could use more colours than this, or just one colour – the choice is yours. Each layer of tulle measures 90 x 15cm (36 x 6in).

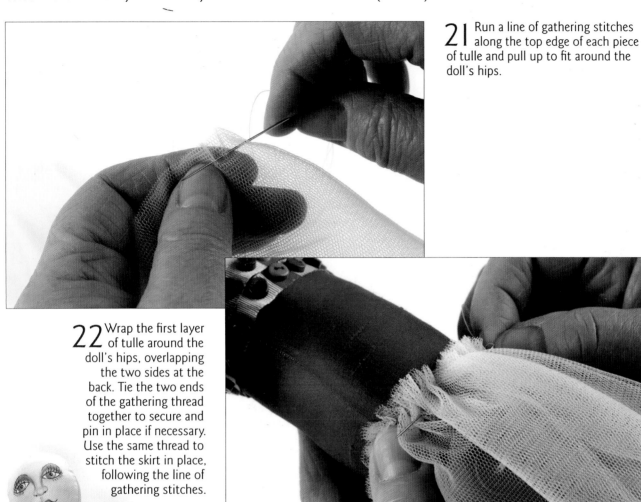

21 Run a line of gathering stitches along the top edge of each piece of tulle and pull up to fit around the doll's hips.

22 Wrap the first layer of tulle around the doll's hips, overlapping the two sides at the back. Tie the two ends of the gathering thread together to secure and pin in place if necessary. Use the same thread to stitch the skirt in place, following the line of gathering stitches.

23 Attach the other two layers of yellow tulle in the same way, followed by the red layer.

24 Take a piece of multi-coloured dyed habotai silk measuring 90 x 35cm (36 x 14in). Tear off two strips each 90cm (36in) long and 5cm (2in) wide for the sleeve trim. Fold the remaining 25cm (10in) strip in half lengthways. Hold the two long edges together by running a gathering thread along them. Pull up the gathering thread and fit the silk on to the doll's hips, just above the tulle. Pin it in place and stitch firmly.

25 The last layer is made from silver net. This is a strip measuring 50 x 8cm (20 x 3in). Fold the net in half lengthways and gather it along the folded edge on to the doll's hips, as with the previous layers. Stitch it firmly in place.

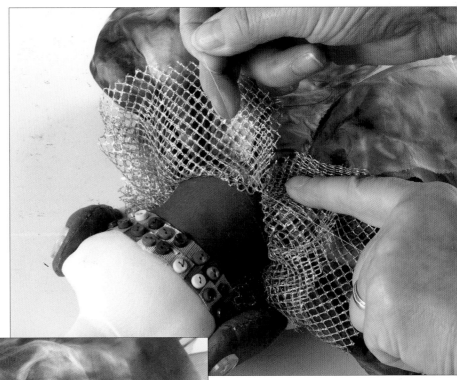

26 Pin a single strip of the striped ribbon over the top edge of the net and stitch it in place. Sew on buttons to match the bodice trim, passing the thread right through the body to attach a button on either side as before.

Frills around the arms and shoulders

There are two silk frills that go around the elbows made with the pieces retained from the skirt, and two frills in each colour of tulle. Two of these go around the elbows with the silk and two around the shoulder joint.

27 Cut two strips of red tulle 5cm (2in) wide. Fold each strip in half along its length so that it is 2.5cm (1in) deep and stitch the two long edges together by running a gathering thread along them. For each strip, pull the thread to gather the tulle into a frill and fit it between the arm and the shoulder. Pull the thread tight and tie it in a knot under the arm to secure. Trim off the ends of the thread.

28 Cut two strips of yellow tulle the same size as the red ones in step 27, and fold and gather them in the same way. Fit one yellow strip around each elbow to hide the stitching on the arm, pull the gathering thread tight and tie it in a knot. Use the same thread to secure the frill with two or three small stitches if necessary. Take the two strips of habotai silk you put by earlier, fold each one in half lengthways and again run a gathering thread along the two cut edges. For each one, pull up the thread to create a frill and place it around the elbow below the yellow one. Secure with a knot and two or three stitches if needed.

Hair

For the hair I have combined two types of fancy yarn in bright reds, yellows, pinks, oranges, purples and blues. The yarns I have chosed are a soft, bobbly, chenille-type yarn and a feathery eyelash yarn.

29 Take the ends of both balls of yarn and wind them around a book or DVD case to make a loose hank of mixed yarn about 25cm (10in) long. Spread this to around 6cm (2¼in) in width.

30 Cut through one side of the hank using a large pair of sharp scissors.

31 Machine stitch across the middle of the hank two or three times using large stitches.

32 Place the hair on the top of the head with the stitched line in the centre running front to back as a parting. Pin and then stitch the hair in place with a few holding stitches.

33 Trim the top layers of the hair using a large pair of sharp scissors to give it a more rounded shape.

Finishing touches

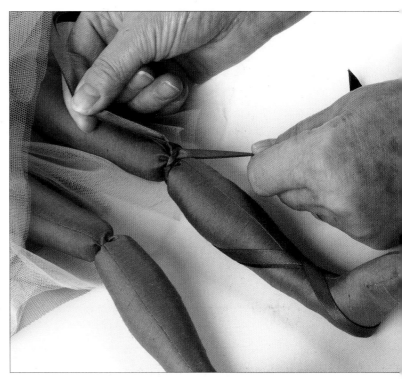

34 Cut a strip of silver net and another of red tulle and tie them each in a bow around the doll's head. Take a length of thin purple ribbon and tie it around her neck, securing it at the back with a few tiny stitches.

35 Take two lengths of each colour ribbon 70cm (28in) long. Holding two lengths – one of each colour – together, place the centre of the ribbons under one of the doll's feet, criss cross them at the ankle and take them round the back of the leg up to the knee. Tie them at the knee and catch with a stitch and a small button to secure.

36 Decorate the other leg in the same way. Trim the ribbons leaving long tails and sew on some tiny buttons to hold the ribbons in place at the ankle.

Our first doll, Miranda, is now complete. On the opposite page is an alternative version made from the same templates and instructions but where the fabrics, yarns and ribbons have been changed to create a more subtle, predominantly blue colour scheme. The bodice has been made from a printed cotton. The silver net is omitted and the dyed habotai silk is replaced by patterned tulle in turquoise.

Anastasia

The woodland nymph is a whimsical figure sitting in a reverie contemplating the butterfly on her hand. She is a fixed-pose doll using many materials, some of which can be retrieved from used clothing. She has a four-part head which is needle-sculpted with drawn features. She has individual wired-fingered hands and feet with stab-stitched toes.

Head and face

Make the head and the needle-sculpted face following the instructions on pages 24–27. Put to one side.

You will need

templates (pages 90–91)

flesh-coloured cotton fabric: 0.25m (10in)

batik cotton fabric: 0.5m (20in)

strip of cotton scrim: 20.5 x 46cm (8 x 18in)

old knitted garment with brown ribbing for hair

old piece of knitwear or felt for leaves

gold seed beads

3 x 6mm (¼in) chenille sticks

sewing machine with open-toe quilting foot and new needle

250g (½lb) bag of good polyester stuffing

25.5cm (10in) embroidery hoop

machine embroidery threads

polyester threads for machine stitching in colours to match the fabric

extra strong upholstery thread for jointing

quilting thread for needle-sculpting and closing seams after stuffing

12cm (5in) forceps or hemostats

hand-sewing needles

long doll needles for jointing

long, fine darning needle, size 7

sharp embroidery scissors, fabric scissors and paper scissors

glass-headed pins

chopstick or stuffing tool

finger-turning tools

sharp pencil or mechanical pencil

white pencil (optional)

vanishing fine-line pen

seam sealant (or PVA glue)

face-colouring equipment (see pages 18–19)

textile paints

piece of baking parchment

pink hot-fix Angelina fibres for butterfly

fine beading wire

Ears

2 Take a piece of flesh-coloured fabric, fold it double and draw round two ear shapes using the template provided on page 91.
Use a sharp pencil to ensure a fine line. Machine stitch around the outlines, leaving the opening. Use flesh-coloured thread and very small stitches.

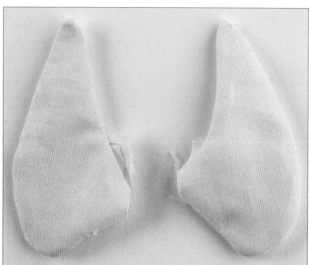

3 Cut out the ears with a 3mm (⅛in) seam allowance. Make the allowance for the opening 6mm (¼in) as it needs to be turned in after stuffing. Turn the ears in the right way and stuff them fairly lightly.

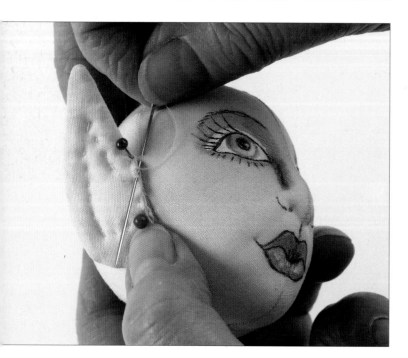

4 Using the vanishing fine-line pen, mark on the inner ear by drawing a faint outline approximately 6mm (¼in) inside each ear. Stab stitch along the line using flesh-coloured thread, leaving a gap level with the opening.

5 For each ear, turn the seam allowance into the opening and stitch it closed. Pin an ear on to each side of the head, laying the stitched opening along the side seam and aligning the top of the opening with the eyes. Stitch the ears in place.

Body

When using batik cotton fabric the colours will vary a lot. You can choose which sections to use for the different body parts before cutting them out. Allow for the body being cut from double fabric and the limbs from a single layer of fabric. Make sure you plan this out so that you have enough fabric.

6 Fold the piece of batik cotton in half on the grain, right sides together. Lay the three template pieces for the body on the fabric with the Lower Front Body on the fold and the grain marks going with the selvedge. Trace around the templates with an ordinary pencil or a white pencil (the white pencil will show up better on a dark fabric). Also mark in the darts.

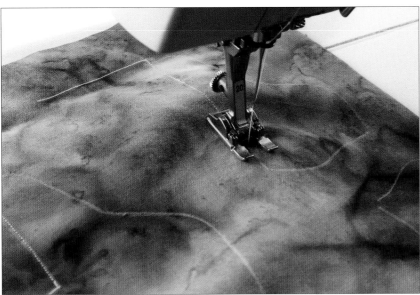

7 Machine stitch along the centre back seam of the Body Back, leaving the opening, and the centre front seam of the Upper Body Front.

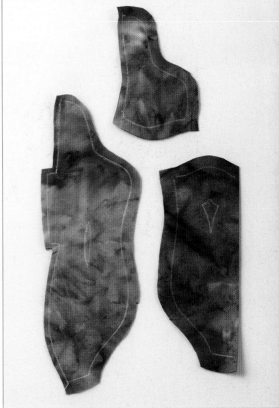

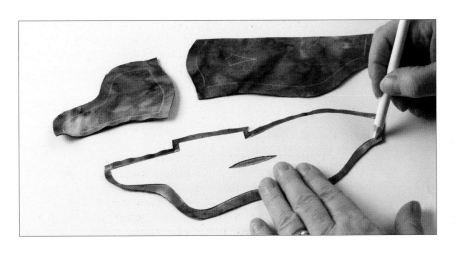

8 Cut out the three body pieces. Leave a 3mm (⅛in) seam allowance on the machined seams and 6mm (¼in) on the other sides that are still to be machined. Do not cut out the darts.

9 Turn the body pieces over and place the paper templates on top. Mark in the darts and the seams on the reverse of each piece of fabric.

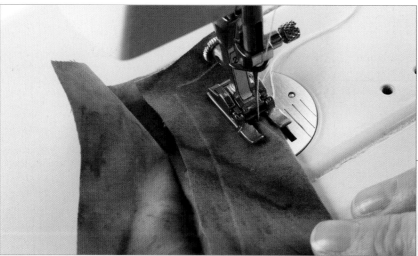

10 Stitch in the darts – two on the Body Back and two on the Lower Body Front.

11 Open out the two Body Front pieces and pin them together, right sides facing, matching the marked sewing lines. Stitch the seam, then trim to 3mm (⅛in).

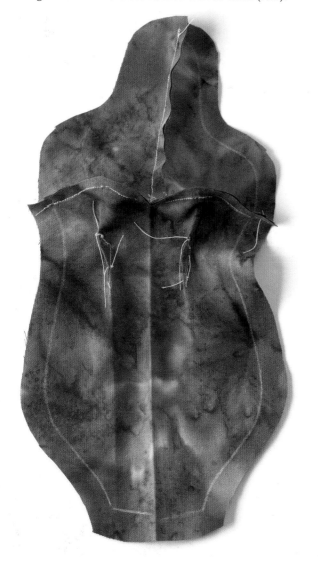

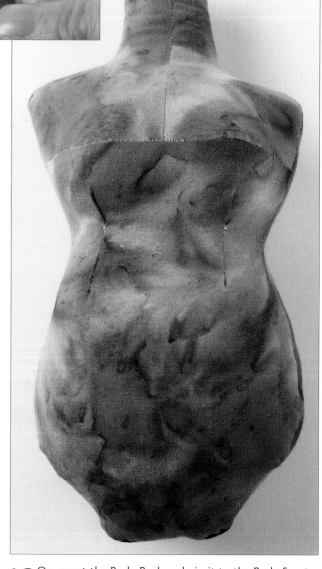

12 Open out the Body Back and pin it to the Body Front, right sides facing, matching the sewing lines. Stitch all around the side seams and trim them to 3mm (⅛in). Use forceps to pull the body right-side out and push around the seams inside to flatten them. Stuff firmly, making sure the neck, the shoulders and the hips are extra firm for holding the head and the limbs (see page 21). Close the back opening with ladder stitch (see pages 40–41).

Arms and hands

The fabric for the arms is first embroidered using free machine embroidery. Transfer the templates and free machine embroider all four pieces before cutting them out. This will be more economical with fabric.

Free machine embroidery

To prepare your sewing machine for free machining, lower the feed dog, remove the presser foot and replace it with a darning foot. There is now no feed to pull the fabric through the machine and you can move the fabric freely underneath the needle. The presser foot lever should be lowered to engage the top tension. The fabric will need to be placed in a hoop to keep it taut while machining, remembering to place it so the back of the fabric lies flat against the machine bed. Now stitch away as you wish. You may find it useful to use a vanishing fine-line pen to draw in the pattern you wish to follow before you start.

13 On a single layer of fabric draw around one arm template piece, then turn it over and draw round it again. Stretch the fabric into a 25cm (10in) embroidery hoop with the drawn shapes in the centre. If you wish, draw your chosen design on to each shape using a vanishing fine-line pen. Thread the sewing machine with your chosen thread and adjust it for free machining (see opposite). Fill each shape with the stitched design, overlapping the marked outlines. I have used a simple leaf design.

14 Repeat step 13 for the other arm. You should now have four embroidered pieces – two for each arm. Cut out all four pieces with a 1cm (½in) seam allowance.

Tip

Make the embroidered design as simple or as complex as you wish. Here I have used a single layer of stitching in one colour to show you how effective a simple design can be. For Anastasia, however, I overlaid three layers of stitching in shades of pink, purple and red.

15 Pin both sides of each arm together with the embroidered sides facing and machine stitch them together along the sewing lines. Leave them open at the wrist. Turn both arms right-side out. Stuff them firmly to about 1cm (½in) from the wrist.

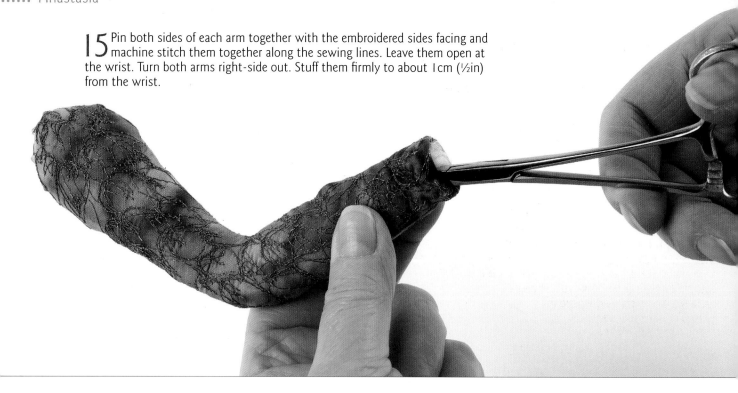

Tip

Make sure the wrists of the hands are narrower than the wrists of the arms so that they slot in comfortably.

16 Make a left and a right hand with individual fingers following the instructions on pages 32–33. Turn in the seam at the wrist of the arm. Push a hand into the end of each arm. Make sure the hands are the right way up and orientated correctly.

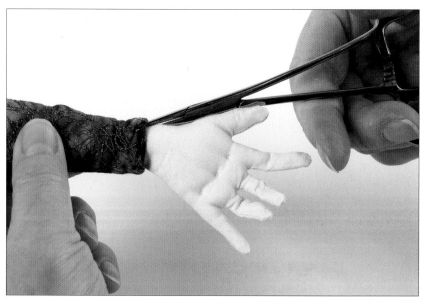

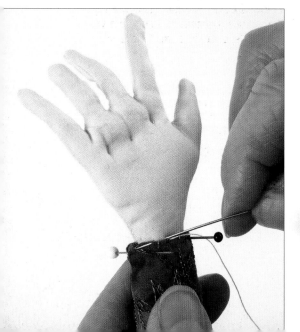

17 Pin then stitch each hand in place using ladder stitch (see pages 40–41).

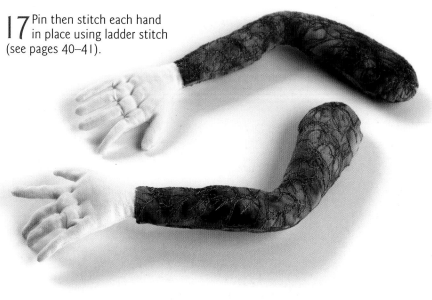

Legs and feet

These are made more or less identically to the arms and hands.

18 Draw out the leg template on a single layer of fabric four times to make a pair of legs, put the fabric in an embroidery hoop and free machine embroider over each leg shape. I have embroidered the legs using green and blue thread – one side of each leg in a different colour from the other. The legs were then constructed and stuffed exactly like the arms. The feet were made following the method shown on pages 34–35 and attached to the legs in the same way as the hands were attached to the arms. Make sure the feet are angled correctly – they should point downwards – and that you have a left and a right leg.

Joining the limbs to the body

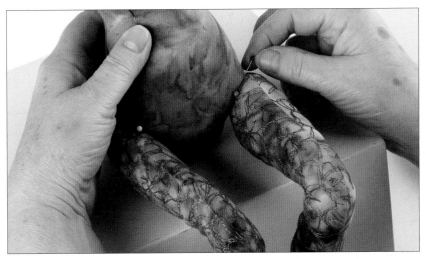

19 Place the doll on a box or a shelf and pin the legs to the body, just below the hips, so that the doll is in a good sitting position. Make sure you pin the legs on the correct sides of the body.

Attaching feet and hands

Always make sure you have a left and a right hand or foot before attaching them to the limbs. Take time to position them so that they look right, then pin them in place before stitching securely. Sew a piece of ribbon or trim around the wrist or ankle to cover the seam if you wish, or add a row of beads.

Hands: push the chenille sticks protruding from the wrist into the arm. Tuck the cotton edge inside the arm and turn under the fabric of the arm at the wrist. Pin then ladder stitch the hand in place.

Feet: feet are not strengthened with chenille sticks, so it is important to achieve a firm ankle. Make sure you have enough stuffing in both the foot and the leg before you join them together. Push all the fabric edges in and join with ladder stitch.

61

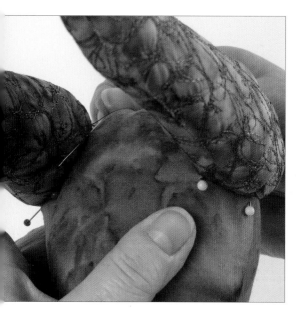

20 When you are satisfied with the position of the legs, stitch them securely in place using ladder stitch.

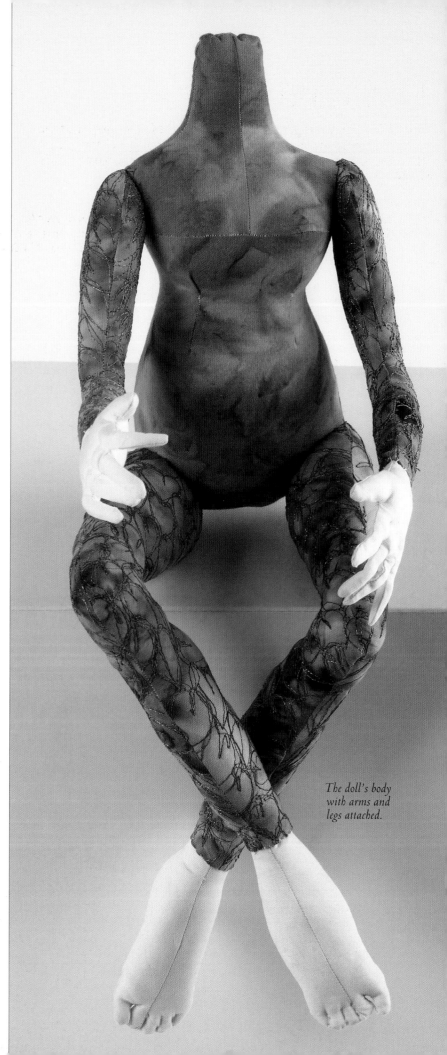

The doll's body with arms and legs attached.

21 With the doll still seated, position the arms and pin them to the body so that the tops of the arms are level with the shoulders. Ladder stitch them in place.

Costume

Anastasia's clothes are very simple to make, but effective. Begin by taking a piece of scrim and colouring it with textile paints to coordinate with the batik fabric. Tear or cut off some strips to decorate the wrists, ankles, shoulders and hips. The more ragged they are the better.

22 Tear an uneven length of the dyed scrim for the hips. Pin it in folds and gathers around the hips and stitch it in place.

23 Pin another strip unevenly around the shoulders so that it drapes down in a V shape at the front. Stitch it in place.

24 Tie thin strips of scrim around the ankles.

25 Decorate the wrists in the same way.

Making leaves to decorate the body

I have used an old sweater for the leaves and for the hair. You could use any old piece of clothing with a suitable colour and texture. Felt can also be used.

26 Put some green or neutral knitwear into a circular embroidery frame. Free machine stitch approximately thirty different leaf shapes in a variety of designs and using different coloured backgrounds. Set up the machine for free embroidery as described on page 59. Make each leaf 1–1.5cm (½in) long.

27 Cut out each leaf individually, taking care not to cut through any of the stitching lines.

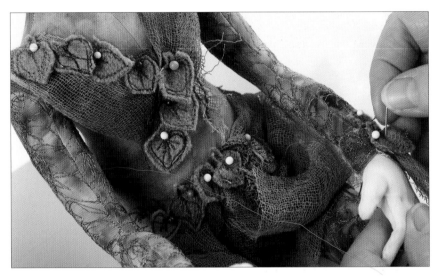

28 Pin the leaves on to the doll's costume – around the hips, across the body and at the ankles and wrists. Position them so that they hang downwards and overlap them slightly.

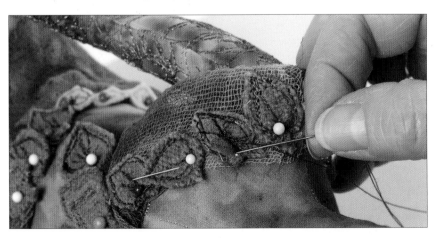

29 When you are happy with the result, stitch each leaf in place with one or two small stitches through the stem. These will be hidden by the beads that are attached later.

30 Using a fine needle or beading needle, bring the thread through the stem of one of the leaves and thread on five or six gold seed beads. Take the thread down through the fabric to form a loop and bring it up through the stem of the next leaf along. Repeat this process until as many leaves as you wish are decorated with beads.

31 To finish, decorate the shoulders with two or three loops of gold seed beads of varying lengths. Paint the finger and toe nails using a Micron Pigma pen in red.

The completed costume, front and back views.

Attaching the head

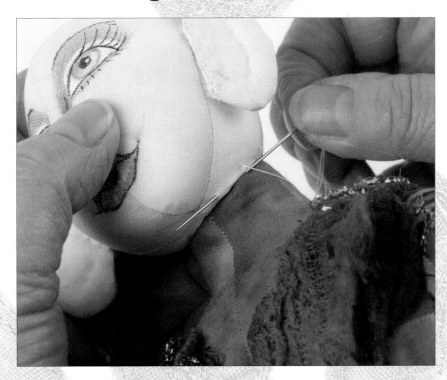

32 Push a space into the back of the head at the back opening. Push the neck into this space, or lever it in using forceps. Pin the head in place while making sure it is correctly positioned. Ladder stitch to secure the head to the neck using flesh-coloured thread.

Hair

The hair is made from three strips of ribbing cut from an old brown sweater.

33 Cut a piece of ribbing 20cm (7¾in) wide and 12cm (4¾in) long, with the ribbing running lengthways.

34 Fold the ribbing in half across the ribs and pin it around the head, with the fold level with the tips of the ears.

35 Stitch the hair in place along the fold using brown thread.

36 Snip along the lines of ribbing up to about 1cm (½in) from the fold to create strips 1cm (½in) wide around the head.

37 Cut another piece of ribbing, this time 18cm (7in) wide and 12cm (4¾in) long with the ribs running lengthways. Fold it in half as before and secure it just above the first layer of hair. Snip along the lengths of ribbing.

38 Cut the last piece of ribbing 12cm (4¾in) long and 10cm (4in) wide with the ribs running lengthways. Fold it into a piece 12 x 5cm (4¾ x 2in). Pin it on top of the head with the fold at the back and covering the top part of the other two layers of hair. This will be the fringe.

39 Stitch the hair in place across the top of the head. Snip along the ribbing as before. Using a fine needle and thread, lay a length of gold seed beads over the top of the head. Take the thread back under the hair and repeat two or three times to create a decorative gold hairband. Secure the thread under the hair.

The butterfly

Begin by preparing a solid sheet of pink Angelina (see the instructions below).

40 Draw around the template provided on page 91 using a vanishing fine-line pen and cut out the butterfly shape.

41 Bend the wings up slightly and over-sew a double length of fine beading wire along the middle of the butterfly. Separate the ends of the wire to make the antennae and curl them over at the tips using forceps. Twist the folded end of the wire together to make the body.

42 Pin and then stitch the butterfly to Anastasia's hand.

Heat-fusing Angelina fibres

Take a small clump of hot-fix Angelina fibres.

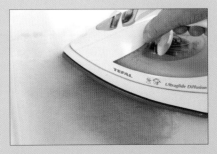

Place it between two sheets of baking parchment and press with a hot iron.

The fibres fuse into a solid mass.

Anastasia the wood nymph is now completed. On the opposite page is shown another version of the wood nymph made from exactly the same template and instructions. She has been made from two different coloured batik fabrics and, to keep her simple, the free machine embroidery has been left out. Dyed scrim has been used to decorate the body and then embellished with some buttons in complementary colours. All the little decorative leaves and beads have been left out to make this doll easier to make.

Titania

This doll is the most complex of the three. I have made her with dupion silk that has been block printed with purple and gold (Jacquard Lumiere) textile paint. If you wish to print your fabric in this way, this should be done before cutting the fabric. Instead of dupion silk, any firmly woven cotton/silk fabric can be used. The fairy has wings made from hot-fix Angelina fibres as well as a beaded tiara and bead embroidery.

Head

Make a four-part needle-sculpted head with a drawn and coloured face as on pages 24–27.

You will need

templates (pages 92–95)

flesh-coloured cotton fabric: 0.25m (10in)

purple and gold printed cotton or silk for body, upper legs and bust: 0.25m (10in)

cotton or silk fabric for lower legs:
20 x 40cm (7¾ x 15¾in);
upper arms: 20 x 40cm (7¾ x 15¾in);
lower arms: 15 x 30cm (6 x 11¾in)

small piece of fabric for gussets

piece of tulle for skirt: 0.5m (20in)

20g (¾oz) ball of wool tops and 20g (¾oz) ball of textured fancy yarn for hair

pink polyester organza for wings: 0.5m (20in)

2 x 7g (¼oz) hot-fix Angelina fibres for wings

24-gauge silver beading wire: approximately 3m (120in) for wings and tiara

12 x 12mm two-hole buttons

silver and pink/purple seed beads for arms and legs

4mm beads for trim and tiara in purple, white and blue

narrow gold ribbon for wrists and ankles

3 x 6mm (¼in) chenille sticks

sewing machine with open-toe quilting foot and new needle

250g (½lb) bag of good polyester stuffing

machine embroidery threads

polyester threads for machine stitching in colours to match the fabric

extra strong upholstery thread for jointing

quilting thread for needle-sculpting and closing seams after stuffing

12cm (5in) forceps or hemostats

hand-sewing needles

long doll needles for jointing

long, fine darning needle, size 7

sharp embroidery scissors, fabric scissors and paper scissors

glass-headed pins

chopstick or stuffing tool

finger-turning tools

sharp pencil or mechanical pencil

white pencil (optional)

vanishing fine-line pen

piece of baking parchment

seam sealant (or PVA glue)

face-colouring equipment (see pages 18–19)

tea light

Body

For the body, I have used a piece of dupion silk block printed following the method described on page 15. You can print any design you wish on to the silk, or alternatively use a piece that already has a design printed on it. Before cutting the body pieces, you will need to join the block-printed silk to a piece of flesh-coloured cotton.

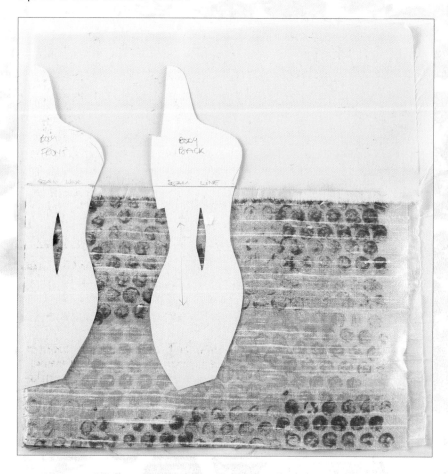

2 Cut a piece of flesh-coloured cotton 32 x 10cm (12½ x 4in) and a piece of fabric for the body 32 x 20cm (12½ x 7¾in). Seam them together along the 32cm (12½in) side and press the seam away from the flesh-coloured cotton. Fold the fabric in half with the right sides together and the seam running widthways. Place the body template pieces on the fabric with the marked seam line aligned with the seam. Place the Body Front on the fold. Draw around both pieces using a sharp pencil and mark in the darts.

3 Machine stitch along the centre back seam on the Body Back, leaving the opening for stuffing. Cut out both pieces with a 3mm (⅛in) seam allowance on the machined seam and 6mm (¼in) on the other sides that are still to be machined. Do not cut out the darts.

4 Machine the darts on the back and front body pieces.

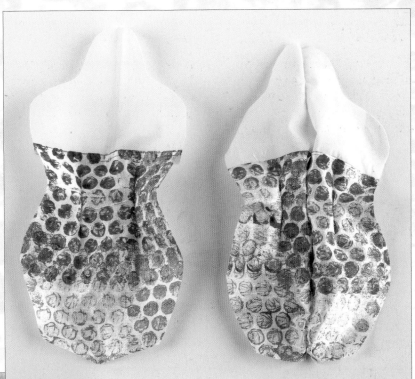

The front and back body pieces.

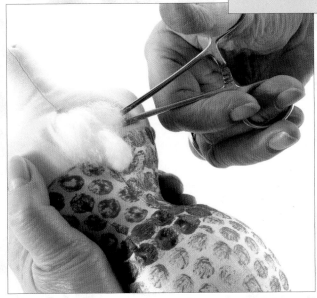

5 Pin the back and front body pieces right sides together with the bodice seams matching and machine around the side seams using small (size 1–2) stitches. Turn right-way out using the forceps and smooth out the seams with a chopstick. Stuff the body firmly, especially the neck, shoulders and hips. These parts take the strain of jointing and holding the head and need to be strong. When the body is firm enough, pin the opening together and close with ladder stitch.

Bust

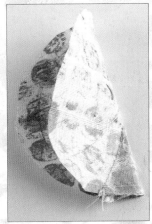

6 With a sharp pencil, draw around the pattern piece twice on a single layer of silk fabric. Cut around each shape, without cutting into the dart, with a 6mm (¼in) seam allowance. Machine in the darts.

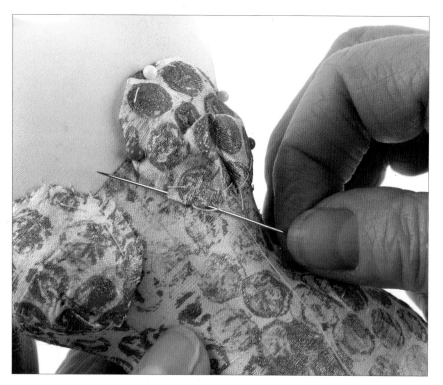

8 Stuff the bust evenly on both sides using forceps and close the opening. Remove the tacking stitches.

7 Finger press the 6mm (¼in) seam to the inside of each cup and tack it down. Pin each cup on to the front of the doll so that the darts match those on the body. Position the cups symmetrically and lying partly over the horizontal seam line. When you are happy with its appearance, ladder stitch the bust in place leaving a space for stuffing.

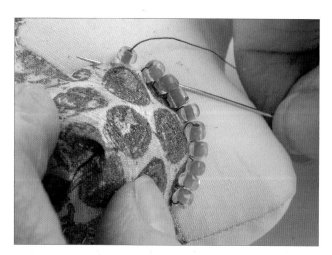

9 Sew 4mm purple beads around the top of each cup. Work in ladder stitch, threading a bead on to each stitch as you work.

The completed body.

Arms and hands

The arms are made in two pieces using a different fabric for the upper and lower arms, with a tab joint at the elbow cut from the same fabric as the upper arms. The finished hand is inserted at the wrist and ladder stitched in place.

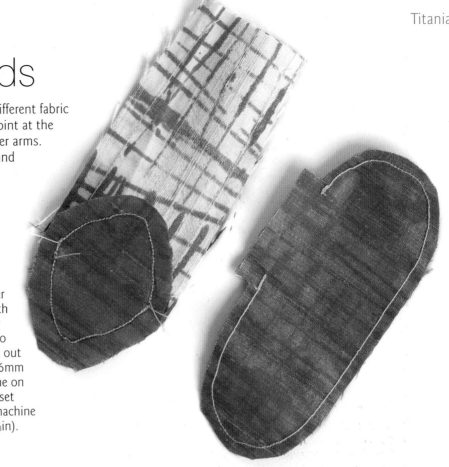

10 On doubled fabric mark out two upper arms, two lower arms and the arm gusset. Machine stitch around the two upper arms leaving the opening. Cut them out with a 3mm (⅛in) seam allowance. For the lower arms, machine stitch the side seams down to the dashed line shown on the template. Cut out the lower arms and the two gussets with a 6mm (¼in) seam allowance. Mark the stitching line on both gussets using a sharp pencil. Pin a gusset on to the two flaps of each lower arm and machine stitch it in place. Trim the seams to 3mm (⅛in).

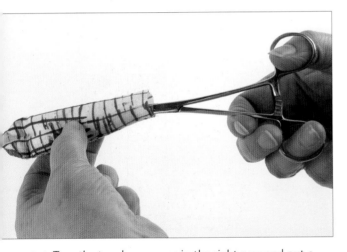

11 Turn the two lower arms in the right way and put a few stitches by hand along the bottom of each tab (marked with a dashed line on the template). This is to prevent stuffing from being pushed into the gusset tabs. Smooth the seams with a chopstick or forceps and stuff the lower arms to about 1cm (½in) above the wrist.

12 Make a right and a left five-fingered hand following the instructions on pages 32–33. Make sure the wrists of the hands are narrower than the wrists of the arms so that they slot together comfortably. Turn the seam allowance for each arm wrist into the arm, then insert the hands, pushing the chenille sticks up into the arm firmly. Make sure the hands are positioned correctly before ladder stitching them in place.

13 Turn the two upper arms in the right way, smooth the seams and stuff firmly. Close the opening with ladder stitch.

Elbow joint

14 Fit the lower arm into the upper arm between the tab joint.

15 Using extra strong thread and a long needle, push the needle through the joint and thread on a button. Take the needle back through the button to secure it and through to the other side of the joint. Fasten a button on that side too, then take the thread through two or three times more to secure and fasten off. Pull the thread tight enough so that there is movement but the joint is held firmly.

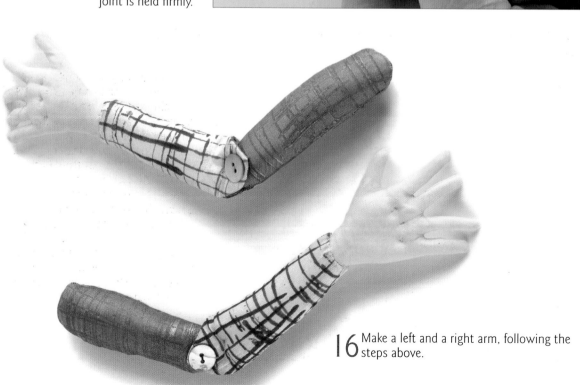

16 Make a left and a right arm, following the steps above.

Legs and feet

Like the arms, each leg is made in two pieces from two different fabrics and tab jointed together. The upper leg is cut from fabric block printed with the same design as the body but using different colours. The lower legs are shaped slightly with a calf; make sure this goes at the back when attaching the legs. The feet are made following the instructions on pages 34–35 and attached in the same way as the arms.

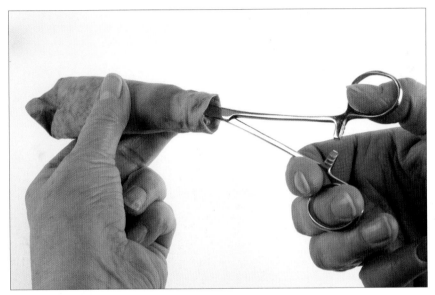

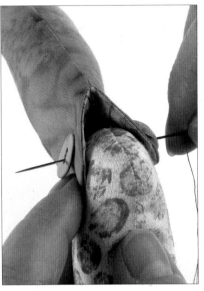

17 Make the lower legs in the same way as the lower arms. Use a contrasting fabric for the gussets. Stitch by hand across the top of the tab joint and stuff each leg firmly to about 1cm (½in) above the opening. Avoid pushing stuffing into the tab joint. Make the feet (see pages 34–35), ensuring the ankles have enough stuffing to be firm. You may need to add more stuffing before finally ladder stitching together.

18 Make the two upper legs and join them to the lower legs with a tab joint (see the instructions for making the elbow joint opposite).

Attaching the legs to the body

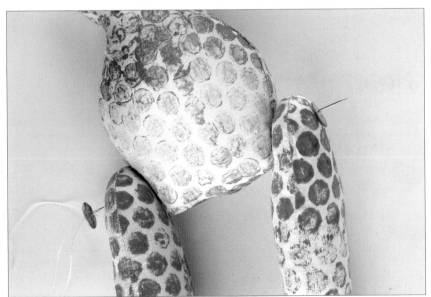

19 Use a 1m (40in) length of extra strong thread and a 19cm (7½in) doll jointing needle. Fasten the thread securely to the side seam at the hip on one side of the doll. With a button on the outside of each leg, go through the leg, button, back through the button and leg, and through the hip to come out in exactly the same position on the other side. Repeat the process, then take the needle back through to where you started and repeat twice more. Pull the thread firmly each time you go through the body so that the legs are jointed firmly.

Attaching the arms to the body

20 The arms are attached to the shoulders using a button joint following the same method as for the legs. This will allow movement of the arms.

Skirt and shoulders

From the two colours of tulle, cut six to eight pieces in each of the three sizes (marked A, B and C on the templates). I have singed the edges of the tulle, which gives a very pretty finish to each piece.

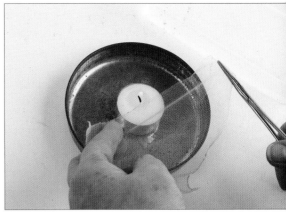

21 To singe the edges of the tulle, use a tea light placed on a saucer and have a bowl of water nearby in case of accidental flames. Light the tea light. Hold a piece of tulle with forceps at one end and by hand at the other and pull it through the bottom of the flame to create an attractive edge. Practise with a spare piece of tulle first.

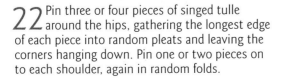

22 Pin three or four pieces of singed tulle around the hips, gathering the longest edge of each piece into random pleats and leaving the corners hanging down. Pin one or two pieces on to each shoulder, again in random folds.

23 Stitch the tulle in place at the shoulders and hips, threading on some 4mm purple beads as you work to decorate. Put two or three beads on to the thread and pull into a circle, then stitch to the hips or shoulders where desired.

Attaching the head

See the instructions on page 29 for attaching the head to the body.

24 Remove the pins from the head opening and make a space in the stuffing. Push the head into the space and adjust it into a good position. Pin the head in place, pushing the seams of the opening inwards. Use ladder stitch to attach the head firmly and securely.

Decorating the body

25 Stitch silver seed beads randomly over the lower arms and attach a band of gold ribbon around the wrist. Colour the finger and toe nails using a pink Micron Pigma pen.

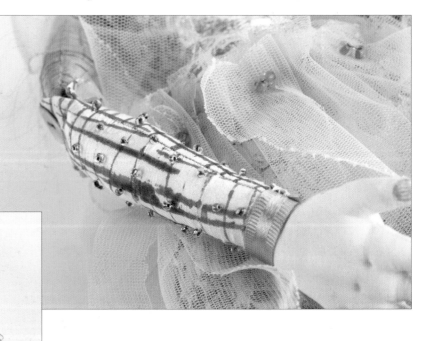

26 Repeat on the lower legs using pink and purple seed beads. Wrap gold ribbon around the ankles and secure with stitches.

Hair

27 Cut a length of wool tops into three or four equal lengths and tease them into one mass.

28 Wind a hank of fancy yarn around a book or DVD case, cut through the hank at both ends and lay the lengths of yarn on to the wool tops in a random fashion. Cut thin strips of the fabrics used to make the doll and some strips of tulle. Lay these on to the other fibres to make the hair. Spread out the yarns and fabrics so that the bundle measures about 8cm (2in) across the middle, where the centre parting will be.

29 Machine stitch across the centre of the hank of yarns twice to hold them together securely.

30 Position the hair on the doll's head, with the machine stitching running front to back along the middle like a centre parting. Pin and then hand stitch it in place along the line of machining.

Tiara

31 Take a 20cm (7¾in) length of fine wire and thread it with 4mm purple, blue and white beads. Leave 5cm (2in) at each end bare, and bend the beaded section into three loops.

32 Attach the tiara to the top of the doll's head by embedding the ends of the wire into the hair.

Wings

The wings are made from heat-fused Angelina fibres. See page 69 for instructions on how to make these. You will need to make two lower and two upper wings. To ensure you have enough Angelina, place two template pieces (one upper and one lower wing) on to baking parchment and cover with teased-out Angelina fibres in a mix of colours. Fold over the baking parchment so the Angelina is covered on both sides and press with a hot iron until the fibres are fused together. Remove the top baking sheet. Repeat for the other two wings.

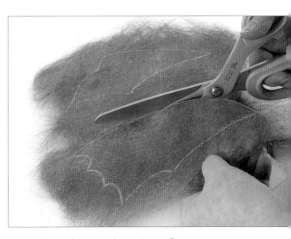

33 Place the template pieces for an upper and a lower wing in the best position on the fused Angelina. Draw around the patterns with a white pencil or vanishing fine-line pen. Cut out the pieces. Do the same again so that you have two of each type of wing.

34 Place one of the wings on to pink organza and lay it under the sewing machine. Set the machine to zig-zag stitch and thread it with a purple machine embroidery thread to match the wings. Take a length of beading wire and zig-zag stitch the wire in place all around the edge of each wing. Repeat for the other three wings.

35 Prepare the sewing machine for free machine embroidery (see page 59). Trim off the excess organza around the edges of the wings and draw on the lines for the veins using a vanishing fine-line pen. Make the two left-hand wings mirror images of those on the right. Use free machine embroidery to stitch along the veins. Now you have two pairs of wings for your fairy.

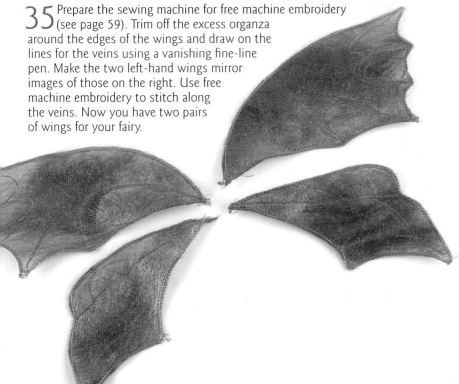

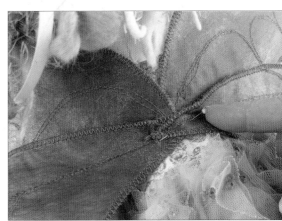

36 Arrange the wings on Titania's back and pin then stitch them in place.

Titania the fairy is now completed. My alternative fairy on the opposite page is made from the same templates and instructions. By using patterned and plain cotton fabrics acquired from a patchwork and quilting shop, no printing or dyeing was involved. The colours used are deeper and more jewel-like, giving the doll a completely different look.

Templates

All the templates in the book are actual size. You can trace them on to copy paper or photocopy them on to card. They are then cut out carefully and accurately so that you can trace around them on to the fabric. Card patterns can be re-used and will last a long time. They are also a little firmer to draw around.

Miranda

Pages 38–53.

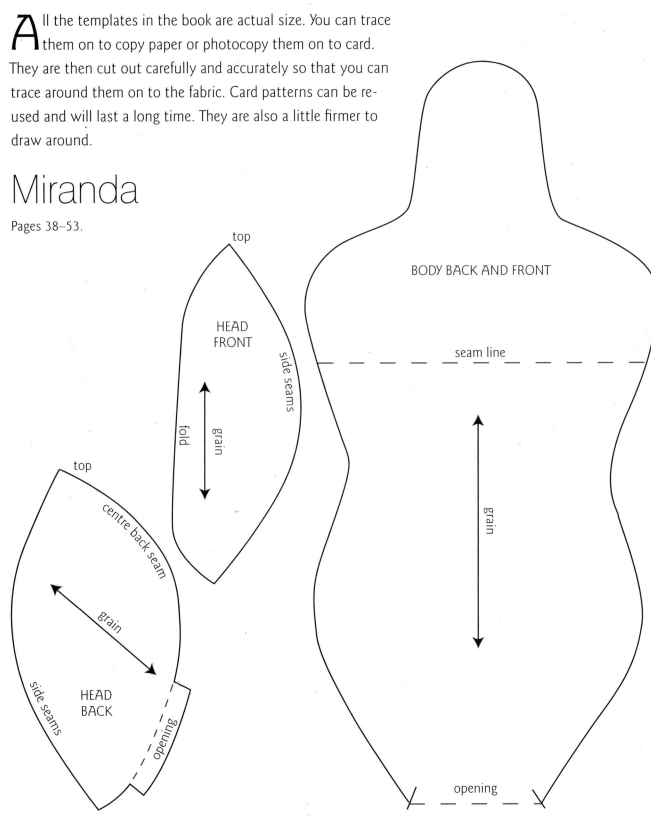

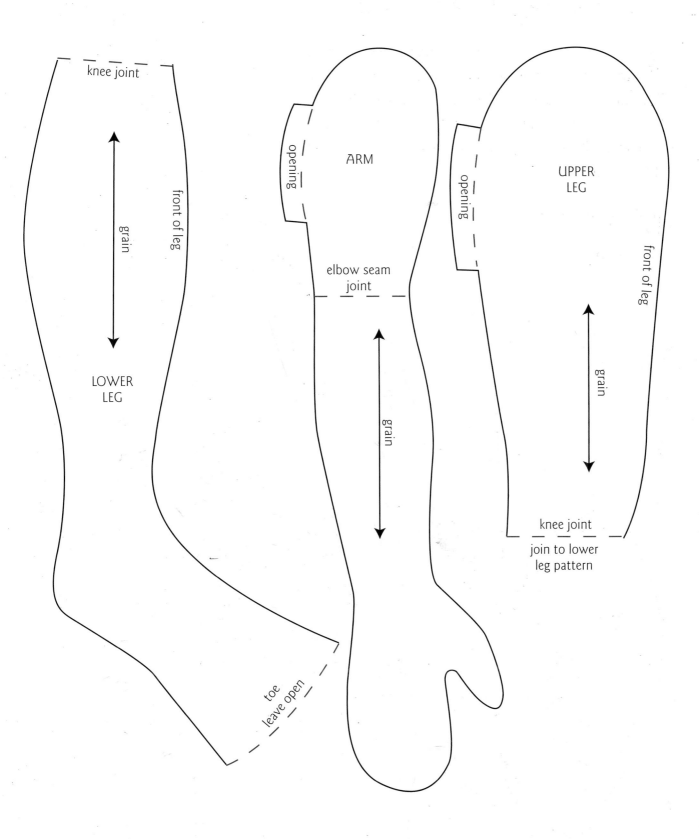

knee joint

grain

front of leg

LOWER LEG

toe
leave open

opening

ARM

elbow seam
joint

grain

opening

UPPER
LEG

front of leg

grain

knee joint

join to lower
leg pattern

Anastasia

Pages 54–71.

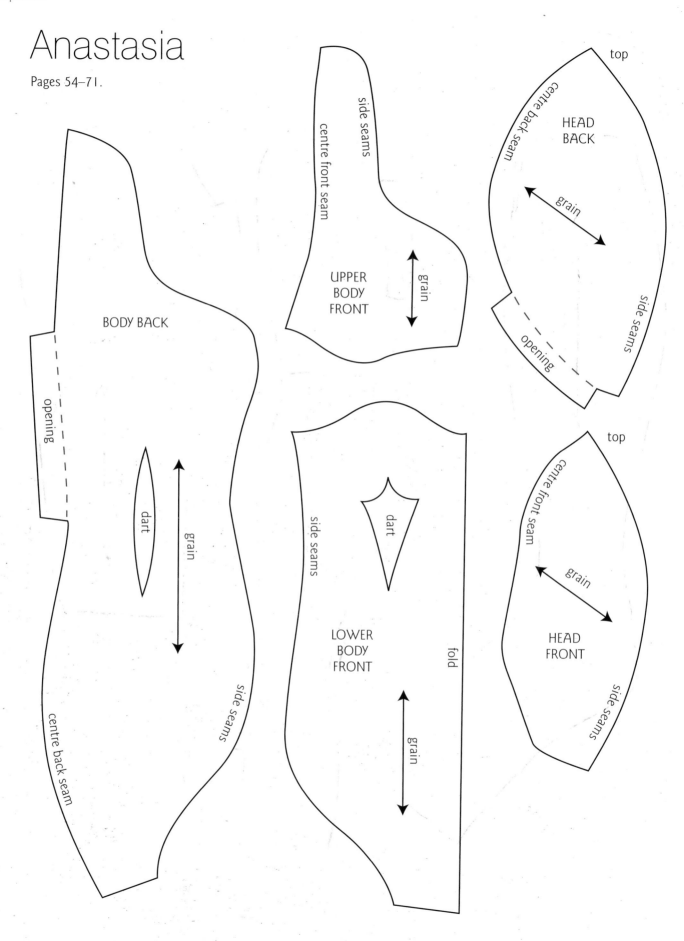

BODY BACK

opening

dart

grain

centre back seam

side seams

UPPER BODY FRONT

side seams

centre front seam

grain

HEAD BACK

top

centre back seam

grain

side seams

opening

LOWER BODY FRONT

side seams

dart

fold

grain

HEAD FRONT

top

centre front seam

grain

side seams

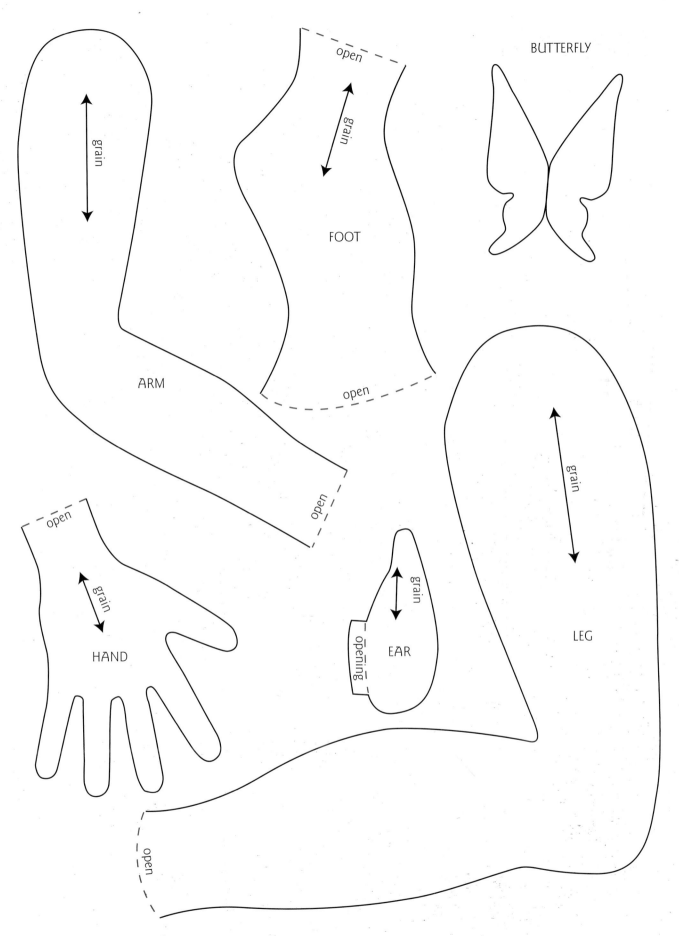

BUTTERFLY

FOOT

open

ARM

grain

open

open

HAND

grain

open

opening

EAR

grain

LEG

grain

open

Titania

Pages 72–87.

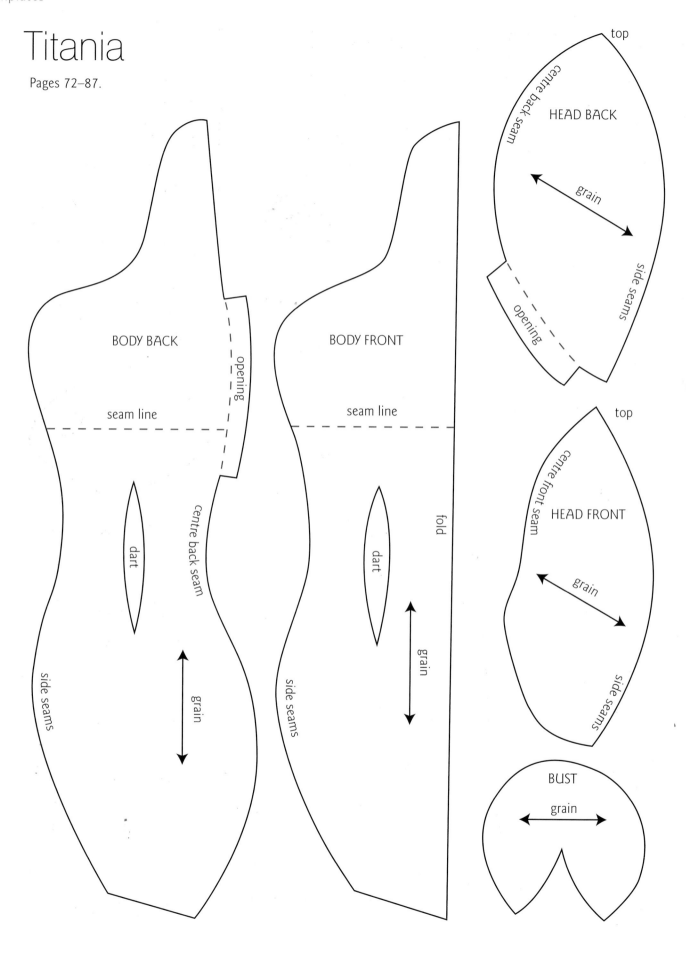

BODY BACK

opening

seam line

dart

centre back seam

side seams

grain

BODY FRONT

seam line

dart

fold

grain

side seams

HEAD BACK

top

centre back seam

grain

side seams

opening

HEAD FRONT

top

centre front seam

grain

side seams

BUST

grain

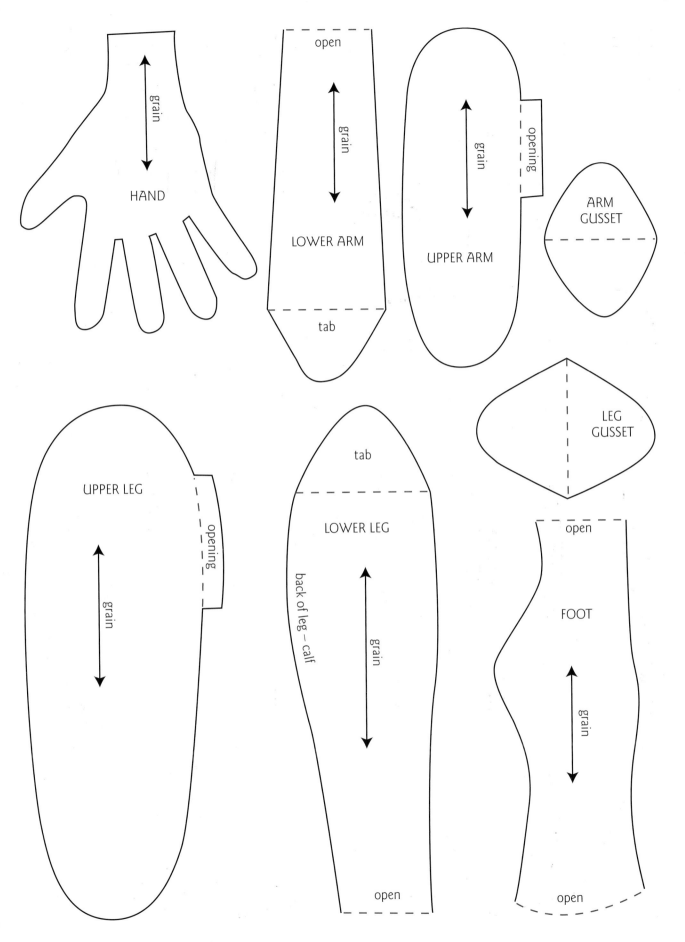

HAND

open

grain

LOWER ARM

tab

grain

opening

UPPER ARM

grain

ARM GUSSET

UPPER LEG

opening

grain

tab

LOWER LEG

back of leg – calf

grain

open

LEG GUSSET

open

FOOT

grain

open

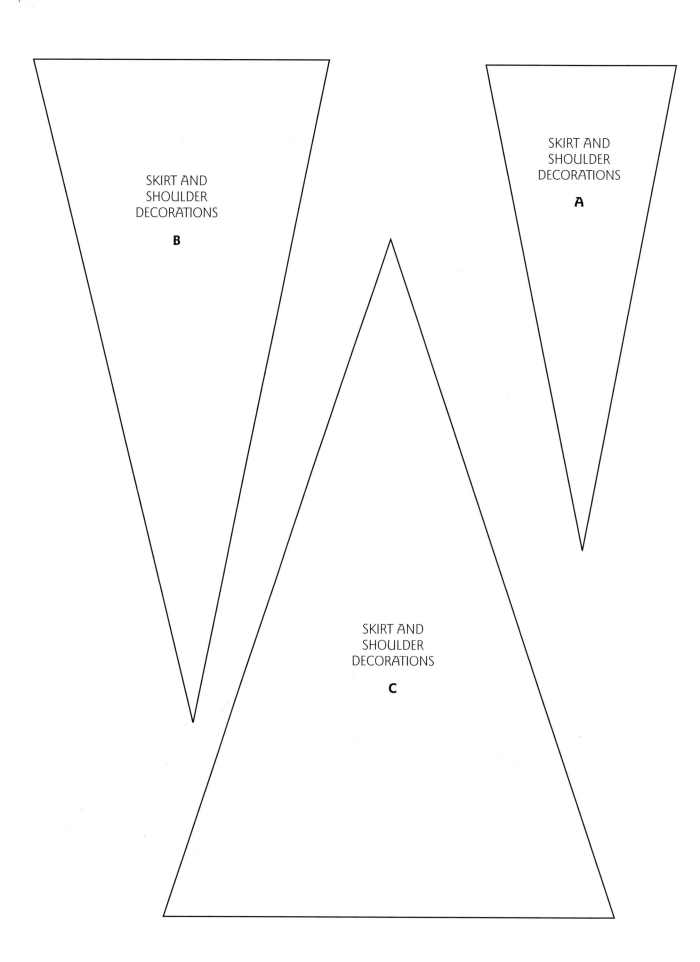

SKIRT AND
SHOULDER
DECORATIONS

A

SKIRT AND
SHOULDER
DECORATIONS

B

SKIRT AND
SHOULDER
DECORATIONS

C

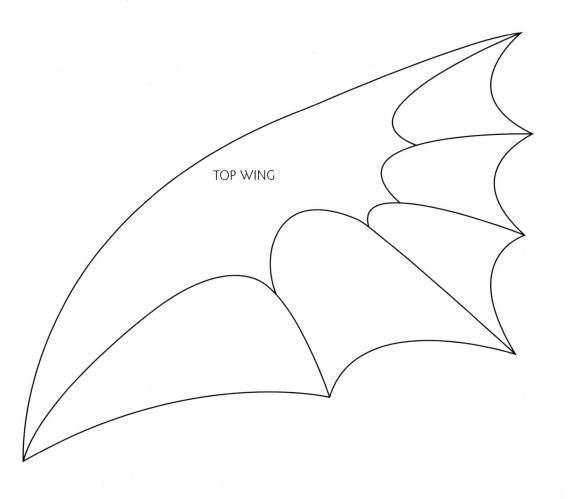

TOP WING

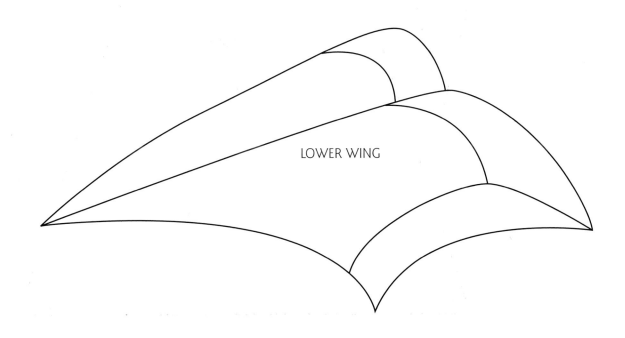

LOWER WING

Index

Online resources to take you further

Every **DIRECTIONS** book comes complete with **additional online resources** to enhance your learning

www.oxfordtextbooks.co.uk/orc/directions/

 online resource centre

www.oxfordtextbooks.co.uk/orc/davis_directions4e/

Visit the website for access to the specific resources.

FOR STUDENTS

* Updates on legislation and case-law

* Annotated web links

* Guidance in answering the problem and essay questions at the end of each chapter

* Multiple choice questions

* Glossary of human rights terms

* Full text of the Human Rights Act 1998

See the Guide to the Online Resource Centre on p. viii for full details.